VISITORS TO THE LAKE DISTRICT are invited to call and in

MAWSON BROTHERS' NURSE

Situated at WINDERMERE and also at BOWNESS, the latter being
within two minutes walk from the Steamer Pier.

VIEW IN THE BOWNESS NURSERY.

**The Stock, which is regularly transplanted and in the finest condition,
includes the following :**

Hardy Conifers in great variety, including all the sorts which visitors admire in Lakeland gardens.

Hardy Trees in various sizes for Park and Avenue planting.

Old-fashioned Hardy Flowering Shrubs, including Lilacs, Mock Orange, Weigelas, Syringas, Ribes, Guelder Rose, Snowberry, &c.

Rhododendrons and Azaleas. Many thousands of plants in all the best varieties to select from.

Hardy Perennials and Florists' Flowers. A special department is made for this class of plants, which are grown in large quantities, and all the best varieties. These include the best Carnations, Delphiniums, Phloxes, Pyrethrums, Pæonies, Perennial Sunflower, &c. As large quantities are grown in pots, orders can be executed at any time.

Hardy Climbers and Roses in great variety and for all purposes. Also old-fashioned and scarce Single and Double Roses, Sweet Briars, Austrian Briars.

Dahlias. A fine collection of Dahlias may be seen in flower during July, August and September.

CATALOGUES POST FREE.

Photo by A. Hollis, Barrow.

FURNESS RAILWAY, GENERAL OFFICES, BARROW-IN-FURNESS.

"THE OLD COPPER NOB"—1846.

EXPRESS PASSENGER ENGINE.—1900.

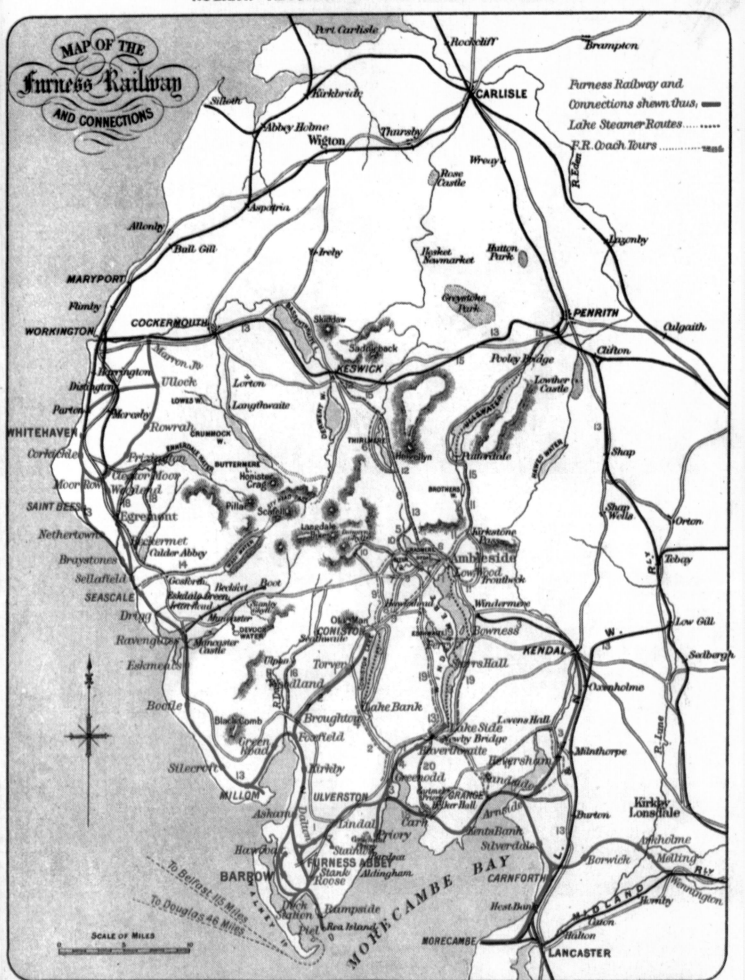

MAP OF THE
Furness Railway
AND CONNECTIONS

Furness Railway and
Connections shewn thus:
Lake Steamer Routes........
F.R. Coach Tours............

THE ILLUSTRATED GUIDE

TO THE

HOLIDAY RESORTS

ON THE

FURNESS RAILWAY.

Illustrating and describing the districts adjoining.

Printed and Published by

W. HOLMES, OTTO PRINTING WORKS, LIGHTBURNE ROAD, ULVERSTON.

The Photographs of Advertisers being supplied by

Mr. Hargreaves, Ulverston; Mr. G. H. Brockbank, Windermere; Mr. G. H Hogg, Kendal; and Mr. Herbert Bell, Ambleside.

THE FURNESS RAILWAY.

A GLANCE at the map shows that the Furness Railway provides the only means of rail communication with the southern and south-westerly parts of the Lake District. The main line runs from Carnforth, along Morecambe Bay, to Whitehaven, on the Cumberland coast, the distance being about seventy-four miles; while a number of branches connect it with various points on the sea, with Coniston Lake and Windermere, and

HIS GRACE THE DUKE OF DEVONSHIRE, K.G., CHAIRMAN OF THE FURNESS RAILWAY.

with other railway systems. It would be difficult to find anywhere in the British Isles another line affording as much charming scenery, the main line skirting the sea shore for almost the entire distance, with the mountains, for which the district is famed, in sight at many points. Probably the only parallel in the country, for wealth of picturesque effects, is the coast section of the Cambrian Railway, where similar conditions prevail as to sea and mountain views. The Furness line, one of the earlier railway enterprises of the country, was opened in 1846, at first running from Dalton to Kirkby and Piel Pier, where the Kirkby slates were exported by vessels. Eventually the mineral riches of the district, especially the hematite iron ore, led to further expansion, while still later enlargements were made to meet the demands of passenger and tourist traffic.

Originally the passenger connection between the Furness system and the country generally was by way of steamers running between Piel and Fleetwood. At the present time, however, the line has ample communication with the railway systems of the country at large, daily, by way of the London and North-Western and Midland Companies at Carnforth, the London and North-Western at Whitehaven, and again at Heversham, near Tebay. We should here mention the important daily service of steamers between Barrow and Belfast, and during the summer months to the Isle of Man, of which the Furness Company, jointly with the Midland Company and

MR. ALFRED ASLETT, SECRETARY AND GENERAL MANAGER OF THE FURNESS RAILWAY.

Messrs. James Little & Co., of Barrow, are owners. The Company have provided, at their Ramsden Dock, extensive accommodation with all modern appliances for these vessels (the trains running alongside the steamer) at the expense of nearly half a million of money, this including the dredging of Piel Bar and other operations of the kind, which enable the Belfast steamers to enter the harbour at any state of the tide. The Bar and Walney Channels are also most efficiently buoyed and lighted. The value of this in the maintenance of "a daily service," and for developing the tourist and passenger traffic with Belfast and the North of Ireland, as well as the Isle of Man, cannot be over-estimated.

The Furness Company, as stated, deal very largely with the mineral productions of the district, and of course with ordinary goods; but a special feature is the provision for passenger

RIGHT HON. LORD MUNCASTER.

VICTOR C. W. CAVENDISH, ESQ., M.P

W. B. TURNER, ESQ.

RIGHT HON. SIR JOHN T. HIBBERT, K.C.B.,
Deputy Chairman.

EDWARD WADHAM, ESQ., J.P.

JAMES W. LITTLE, ESQ., J.P.

The Directors of the Furness Railway Company.

conveyance, notably under the *régime* of the present Secretary and General Manager, Mr. Alfred Aslett. This gentleman has been able to organise a large number of arrangements of great convenience for the tourist and general public, among them the plan of throwing open all the pleasure resorts of the line, during the entire year, at single fares for the return journey, the tickets being available on the day of issue only, and for ordinary trains. Still another arrangement is that of issuing first and third-class weekly tickets between any two stations on the line at the rate of six return journeys for six ordinary single fares. These return journeys can be made at any time during the week, and are greatly appreciated by professional persons, families residing at the seaside, and by the public generally when having to visit the same place several times in the course of the week. But beside these the Company provide a multiplicity of fortnightly, week-end, cheap day, market, cheap day with alternative return routes, and special day tickets for anglers, golfers, tennis players, pleasure parties, and the like, with a magnificent series of circular tours by rail, coach, and lake. These items, amongst many others, we mention to show that the management are fully up-to-date, if not indeed a little ahead of the times, in all matters pertaining to the pleasure, comfort, and convenience of the travelling public.

Of course the Company have not failed to make full provision with a view to enabling the patrons of their line to enjoy the scenery of other portions of the Lake District than those which

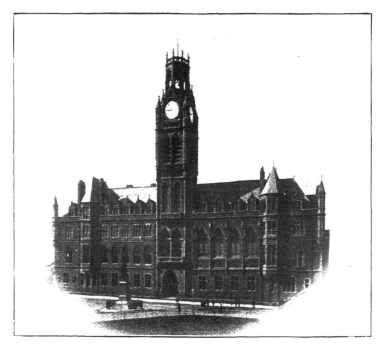

Photo by Hollis, Barrow.   BARROW TOWN HALL.

they immediately traverse. This is by means of the circular tours (by rail, coach, and lake) already mentioned. The Company now offer a choice of twenty or more of these delightful circuits at almost absurdly low prices, the noted "Six Lakes" tour being perhaps the most surprising value for money. It includes Windermere, Rydal, Grasmere, Thirlmere, Derwentwater, and Ullswater, tickets for the entire trip being issued for a fortnight, at the surprisingly low charge of thirteen shillings. Persons familiar with the Lakes will understand the attractions of the trip when we say that the excursionist goes by rail, say from Furness Abbey to the Company's Lake Side station on Windermere, thence by their steam yacht the whole reach of the lake to Ambleside, then by coach to Ullswater, where another steam yacht is in readiness to carry him to Pooley Bridge, after showing him the charms of the "English Lucerne." From this landing he continues his course by coach to Penrith, going by rail (via the London and North-Western) to Keswick, and returning to Ambleside via Thirlmere, Grasmere, and Rydal, by coach, where the Company's steam yacht again receives him and transfers him to the train at the foot of the lake, by which he returns to Furness Abbey. This, as we have said, is merely a typical specimen of the Company's tours, full particulars of which are given in their pamphlet entitled "Tours through Lakeland," excellent maps of each route being provided. Thanks to these efforts put forth on behalf of the public, the passenger bookings have shown a large increase over previous years.

MR. FRANK STILEMAN, M I.C E.,
Chief Engineer.

MR. W. F. PETTIGREW, M.I.C.E., M I.M E.,
Locomotive, Carriage, & Wagon Superintendent.

MR. F. ALFRED CURREY.
Solicitor.

MR. J. MASON,
Accountant.

MR. C. MOSSOP,
Goods Manager.

MR H. BAGOT,
Audit Accountant.

MR. W. S. WHITWORTH,
Resident Engineer.

MR. F. J. RAMSDEN,
Superintendent of Line.

CAPTAIN WARDS,
Harbour Master to Port of Barrow.

Photo by Hollis, Barrow.   H.E. LI HUNG CHANG AT THE BELSFIELD HOTEL, BOWNESS-ON-WINDERMERE, AUGUST, 1896.

Perhaps we may here refer to the recent improvements in rolling stock, etc., made by the Company to meet the demands of the increased traffic of the line in various departments. At the present date a large number of engines of the most efficient and modern type (designed by the locomotive superintendent) are in use, while the carriage stock has been completely revolutionised and brought up to the highest standard of passenger conveyances in the country. It is not too much to say that their "bogie semi-corridors," some of which run over the Midland Railway on different circuits and are handsomely decorated and furnished with views of Furness scenery, can hardly be improved upon for comfort and convenience. One important feature is the employment of the electric light on Stone's system, the current being generated by each carriage independently of the others making up the train. The system is highly efficient and at the same time economical. The train services are very frequent and convenient. It is also noticeable that the stations throughout the system are substantially built and in very tasteful styles, while the permanent structures and engineering works are of the most solid description. The shrubberies at the different stations are a unique and attractive feature. An important adjunct of the Company's facilities is the fleet of steam yachts on Lake Windermere, six of these vessels being in use, while they have also a steam gondola on Coniston Lake. The Company own as well a number of powerful steam tugs in connection with their dock and port business, and we should not omit mention of their handsomely-fitted hotel at Furness Abbey, lit throughout with electric light, and under the management of Messrs. Spiers & Pond, Ltd.

VIEW OF LANDING STAGE AND NEW REFRESHMENT PAVILION, LAKE SIDE.

We have not attempted to do more than show how important a factor the Furness Railway has been in the development of the district. It need not be said that this could hardly have been the case unless the promoters and managers had been men of experience and foresight in matters of the kind. Its present status in this respect is equally fortunate. The Chairman of the Company is his Grace the Duke of Devonshire, K.G., and the Deputy Chairman the Right Hon. Sir John T. Hibbert, K.C.B., late Secretary to the Treasury, and the present Chairman of the Lancaster County Council. Among the Directors, besides the foregoing, are the Right Hon. Lord Muncaster, Victor C. W. Cavendish, Esq., M.P., W.B. Turner, Esq., James W. Little, Esq., J.P., and Edward Wadham, Esq., J.P. (representative of the Duke of Buccleuch). Of the working staff, Mr. Alfred Aslett, the Secretary and General Manager, has had a wide and profitable experience in railway matters, having been Secretary and General Manager to the Cambrian Railways, and Manager to the Eastern and Midland (now Midland and Great Northern Joint) in Norfolk, previously to occupying his present seat. Mr. Frank Stileman, M.Inst.C.E., the Chief Engineer of the Company, and Mr. Mossop, the Goods Manager, have long been connected with the line and docks. M. W. F. Pettigrew, M.Inst.C.E., M.Inst.M.E., is the Superintendent of the Locomotive, Carriage, and Wagon Departments, and Mr. W. S. Whitworth, the Resident Engineer, has been with the Company since 1872. Mr. F. J. Ramsden, the Superintendent of the line, is the only son of the late Sir James Ramsden, whose services to local communities have been mentioned, and other officials have records of long experience in the lines of their respective duties.

THE BRIDGES NEAR ULPHA.   See Circular Tour No. 16, on Back Page of Cover.)

CARNFORTH.

CARNFORTH lies at the north-eastern extremity of Morecambe Bay, 6½ miles from Lancaster. It was formerly a small country village in the parish of Warton, with few inhabitants, and these employed chiefly in the cultivation of the land. Within the last 30 years it has grown into a place of importance, with good shops, long streets of dwelling-houses, and an excellent hotel. The change is due to the iron ore mines in the neighbourhood, and to the extensive smelting works of the Carnforth Hæmatite Iron Company.

CARNFORTH.

These works, which are conspicuous by their tall chimney and great furnace towers comprise six blast furnaces, and are capable of producing 4,000 tons of pig iron per week.

Carnforth is a Station on the London and North-Western and Midland Railways, and is also the terminus at the southern end of the Furness Railway, who run trains in connection with these trunk lines to all parts of the Kingdom.

After the train leaves Carnforth there may be observed, at little distance on the right hand side, the square grey tower of the Parish Church of Warton. This is a spacious building, comprising the tower, nave, side-aisles, and chancel. It is situated at the foot of a rugged limestone elevation called Warton Crag, which bears on its crest the remains of a beacon and of ancient fortifications. The Washingtons, from whom was decended the first President of the United States of America (General Washington), were residents in Warton for many generations,

BORWICK HALL, CARNFORTH.

WARTON, NEAR CARNFORTH.
(The home of the Washington Family.)

THE VISITOR PRINTING COMPANY,

Printers, Stationers, Lithographers, Bookbinders, Tobacconists, Fancy Goods Dealers and Billposters.

THE VISITOR LENDING LIBRARY
(IS THE ONLY ONE IN THE DISTRICT.)

Head Office :—MORECAMBE. CARNFORTH.

An extensive range of business departments is comprised in the establishment successfully conducted by the Visitor Printing Company, whose attractive premises in Market Street are recognised as a depot for Printing, Stationery, Fancy Goods, Tobacco, Newspapers, Periodicals, &c. The shop is centrally situated in the main thoroughfare of the town, and has a double window frontage, one side being utilised for the display of a large assortment of Stationery, Fancy Goods, &c., and other articles of a useful and decorative character suitable for gifts, prizes, &c. The other window is devoted to the Tobacconist's Department and shews a capital selection of pipes, pouches, &c. Printing in all branches from a visiting card to a mammoth poster is undertaken in first-class style at very reasonable charges, and the Firm also do the billposting in the neighbourhood, having all the prominent stations for that purpose. All the principal London and provincial papers, periodicals and magazines are supplied and delivered daily to customers' residences immediately after arrival by the early trains, orders in either of the above mentioned departments receiving prompt and punctual attention. Since the present Firm took over the business from Mr. J. R. Brockbank who formerly carried it on, a Lending Library has been added, and as books are lent out to residents and visitors at the nominal charge of 2d. per volume per week, it goes without saying that the venture is a popular one. This is the only Library in the District.

Mr. C. MACDONALD,

Watchmaker, Jeweller, Optician, etc.,

25, Market Street, CARNFORTH.

Purchasers requiring absolute reliable time-keepers, whether for ordinary or farm

*A Speciality :—Gold filled Spectacles and Eyeglasses with changeable lenses.

work, engine drivers, etc., should certainly be satisfactorily suited at Mr. Macdonald's well-stocked establishment, where he holds one of the largest and most valuable stocks of watches, jewellery, and useful and decorative articles in this line in the district. The business, established about twenty years, is carried on in the compact and well-appointed premises in Market Street, within five minutes' walk of the railway station in the main thoroughfare of the town. The windows present an attractive and tasteful show of high-class goods in silver lever watches from 35/-, hall-marked gold brooches, pins, gold and silver jewellery and a great variety of silver and electro-plated ware, and elegant and useful articles suitable for prizes, presentation and souvenirs. A large assortment of optical goods is also submitted in the best makes of spectacles and folders, which are accurately adjusted to suit all sights.* A popular feature of the business is the sale of 22 carat gold wedding rings, with which a present is given. Mr. Macdonald also makes a speciality of repairs.

The Carnforth Cycle Company.

Manager—

Mr. C. B. DEAN.

Lancaster Road, Carnforth.

The STORMLIGHT

SOME very urgent reasons offered by the Carnforth Cycle Co., for placing orders with them for building machines for the season to come, this being one of the few firms in North Lancashire who may claim to have established a reputation beyond local limits by the consistent excellence of their designs and finished workmanship. The Company was established in 1896, the practical management being entrusted to Mr. C. B. Dean, who takes the personal supervision of the business. The works in Lancaster Road are completely equipped with an up-to-date plant for the various processes of manufacture, including all

branches, in which about eight experienced hands are employed. The leading speciality of their make is the "Stormlight" Cycle, which is pronounced on competent authority to be a thoroughly reliable machine, at a very moderate price, as will be readily testified by hundreds of grateful purchasers, who have repeatedly expressed satisfaction with this elegant and durable model. Repairs are also executed with speed and promptitude, efficient workmanship being guaranteed at reasonable charges, and enamelling is undertaken by the latest hydro-carbon process, which brings out the machine, in every respect, equal to new in appearance,

Mr. M. BRIGGS,

Boot & Shoe Maker,

9, Market Street, CARNFORTH.

The cheapest and best boots and shoes for all seasons and all wears are always to be obtained at "Briggs'" noted warehouse in Market Street, where all the leading lines in the trade are on offer. These include the "Fearnought," "Tredeezie," "Apropos," "Nelson," "Fair Wear" and "Bonafide" brands for which Mr. Briggs is agent, together with the latest novelties in special makes suitable for ladies', gentlemen's and children's wear. The premises, centrally situated in the main thoroughfare of the town, and near the railway station, have an excellent window frontage neatly arranged with a varied assortment of goods, in which may be selected a leading speciality in a reliable make of men's boots at 10 6, and a sturdy workman's boot at from 5 11 the pair. Careful attention is given to repairs, which are carried out on the premises by first-class experienced hands, the best quality of material and workmanship at moderate charges being guaranteed in every case. Orders for measured boots and shoes are also executed on similarly efficient lines.

Mr. WILLIAM PERFECT,

High-Class Tailor,

Bank Buildings, 48, Market Street, CARNFORTH.

now submitted for inspection by Mr. William Perfect, who has exercised his usual care and judgment in the selection of the latest patterns, and in securing the best and most reliable quality of goods for ladies' and gentlemen's tailor-made garment. The establishment forms a portion of Bank Buildings, and is situated close to the railway station and the post office, in the main thoroughfare of the town. The window is dressed in attractive style, and contains samples of woollen and other materials displayed for the inspection of customers. Mr. Perfect is a thoroughly expert cutter, experienced in the higher branches of breeches making, liveries, hunting outfits, and ladies' costumes, mantles, coats, and other garments in all the most fashionable models of the London and Paris season. The trade is entirely confined to the execution of bespoke orders, which are guaranteed the perfection of fit, style and finished workmanship, assured by the close personal supervision of the proprietor in every detail of manufacture.

An excellent choice of new materials, suitable to the requirements of the season, is

Mr. J. KNOWLES,

Upholsterer and General House Furnisher,

Scotland Road, CARNFORTH.

An extensive and well-selected stock of furnishing requisites, for all purposes, is submitted for inspection at the above-named establishment, where Mr. Knowles is always prepared to supply goods of sound and reliable quality, for the equipment of a residence on any scale, on the shortest notice. The premises in Scotland Road have a good window frontage, in which is displayed a great variety of cabinet ware, and articles both useful and decorative; and within the spacious interior is ample room for the storage of the extensive stock of brass and iron bedsteads, bedding, carpets, linoleums, oil-cloths, mail carts, bassinettes, and furniture of every description. A large assortment of paper-hangings in the newest and most artistic designs and shades is also shewn, together with mouldings of the best English and foreign manufacture

for picture-frames, orders for which are carried out, in any style required, by experienced workmen on the premises. Additional storage room is provided on the opposite side of the street, where spacious warehouse premises are

occupied for the purpose.

WASHINGTON HOUSE, CARNFORTH.

SILVERDALE.

A PLEASANT seaside village much frequented by visitors during the summer. The village is about a mile distant from the station. It may be reached by two different roads. That to the left is the shortest and most direct. That to the right is more circuitous, and takes the visitor past the old Church, a plain building erected in 1829. A handsome new Church, dedicated to St. John, was opened in 1886, since which time the old Church has been only used as a mortuary chapel, its graveyard being the parochial burial ground. A high hill to the right is called Castle Barrow. The ascent is worth making, as there is a very extensive view from the summit. A tower standing some distance away, and built upon a precipitous rock facing the bay, is called Lindeth Tower, built by a Preston banker for a residence. From its rocky position it has also received the name of "Gibraltar." Mrs. Gaskill, the well-known authoress, resided for some time at Lindeth Farm, and wrote some of her

VIEW NEAR SILVERDALE.

stories there. Not far from Silverdale, on the Challon Hall Estate, is a fresh-water lake about 30 acres in extent, and in some places nearly 120 feet deep. It is called Hawes Tarn, and its waters are said to be affected by the rise and fall of the tide. It is remarkable for the vast quantity of small univalve marine shells found in its bed. In a field belonging to the same estate there stands a huge boulder-stone, so curiously poised upon a piece of rock that one wonders how it could have been placed there, and how it maintains its position. It is 13 feet high, 10 feet in diameter, and is estimated to be 80 tons in weight.

Shortly before the train reaches Arnside Station, a view is obtained on the left of Arnside Tower, an ancient quadrangular structure standing on the summit of a grassy hill. It was once possessed by the Stanleys, and it was intended, probably, to serve as a watch tower, and also as a means of defence and temporary retreat against the assaults of lawless marauders who infested the coast in search of plunder. It is now roofless and in ruins. It appears to have been four storeys high, with an embattled roof, and was ascended by a spiral staircase of 54 steps, which are still nearly perfect. From the summit fine views are to be obtained over Morecambe Bay, and over the limestone fells of Hutton Roof, Tarleton, and other eminences at a greater distance.

ARNSIDE.

(Passengers change here for the Levens and Heversham Tour, Oxenholme and Kendal)

IS about two miles from Silverdale, and stands close to the sea. Its population has largely increased of late years, proving that the place is growing in public estimation. Most of the houses lie along the shore and on the sides of Arnside Kust. This is a fine headland, forming the most southerly portion of the County of Westmorland. It is 550 feet high, and largely covered with trees. Those who climb to its summit will be amply rewarded for their trouble, for the view to be obtained from it is one of great variety and extent. The inland view embraces, to the north-east, Heversham, with its white Church tower standing conspicuously among the trees, by which

ARNSIDE.

it appears to be surrounded, backed by the range of Howgill Fells and Shap Fells in the far distance; it embraces also Whinfell, above Kendal, Ill Bell and High Street, and more to the west, Kirkstone, Fairfield, and Helvellyn; and, indeed, all the chief mountains of the Lake District. Ingleborough and other Yorkshire hills are seen on the east, and, nearer, Farleton Knot, with the beautiful woods about Beetham and Dallam Tower in the foreground. Lancaster, with its Church and Castle, Carnforth, and other places in the south, while westward, and along the shores of Morecambe Bay, the view embraces Humphrey Head, Grange and Kents

Bank, Holme Island, Chapel Island, and the Hill of Hoad, with Sir John Barrow's Monument on the top, showing the position of Ulverston. Farther off, Piel Castle and the Lighthouse on Walney Island are seen, and the district of Low Furness, and many other objects of interest, the whole forming a panorama which, for extent and beauty, when the day is clear, can scarcely be surpassed. At Arnside there is a diverging branch line, which passes Sandside, Heversham, and Kendal, and proceeds thence to Windermere. Particulars of this line are given in Circular Tour No. 3, on back page of cover. On leaving Arnside the railway crosses the estuary of the river Kent by means of an iron viaduct, 1,300 feet in length. To construct it was a work of great difficulty, in consequence of the great depth of sand—from 30 feet to 70 feet—which made it almost impossible to obtain a sufficiently secure foundation. Between the line and the foot of the hills, on the right, we notice a considerable tract of level land that has been reclaimed from the sea.

Passing on the right edge of Meathop Fell, we cross the Winster, a river which divides Westmorland from the outlying part of Lancashire, and note that, looking up the Winster Valley, the scenery is of a very picturesque description. We notice also that a large tract of land—upwards of 400 acres—has here been reclaimed from the sea. At no great distance from the shore an

SANDSIDE.

isolated hill, conical in shape, and thickly clothed in wood, rises from the plain. It was anciently called Atterpile Castle, and is now called Castlehead. The hill consists of an immense mass of Silurian rock, which ancient Britons, Saxons, Danes, and Norsemen have successfully held as a fortified encampment, as is proved by the numerous coins and other objects belonging to all these nations from time to time found there. John Wilkinson, the great ironmaster of the last century, had his house there, and on the river Winster the model of an iron-built vessel which he designed was constructed and successfully floated in 1786.

On the left is Holme Island, about 10 acres in extent, which the late Mr. A. Brogden, M.P., was the first to take possession of and render habitable. He built a mansion upon it, and planted it with ornamental trees and shrubs, and otherwise embellished it, making it a perfect paradise; and he united it to the mainland by means of a solid embankment, protected on the right side by an embattled wall, and on the left by iron railings, so that it might be accessible at all states of the tide. On the south side of the island is a model of the Temple of Vesta, built in white limestone,

Messrs. JAMES CROSSFIELD & SONS,

Tea Merchants, Grocers and Italian Warehousemen, Provision Merchants, Bakers, Stationers and Tobacconists.

Telegrams: CROSSFIELD, Arnside.   ARNSIDE.   Postal Address: via Carnforth.

Every advantage provided by the modern "Stores" system of trading is afforded by the above-named establishment, which in the range and extent of its business departments, the invariable high-class quality and sterling value of the goods supplied, and the moderate charges prevailing will bear favourable comparison with any stores or house in this line of purveying. The business is of old-established and substantial standing, having been in the possession of the Crossfield family for many years, of whom the present proprietor Mr. James Crossfield has carried on the business for over forty years and it is now under the management of his two sons Messrs. R. G. and J. S. Crossfield. The firms premises, centrally situated within five minutes walk from Arnside railway station, and facing Morecambe Bay, have a wide frontage of some thirty feet, divided into large plate glass windows showing a tasteful display of goods. This is conveniently arranged for the purpose with two long counters for grocery, provisions, Italian warehouse goods, etc., while another portion is devoted to tobacco, stationery and postal business, the establishment being the local post and telegraph office. On the rear of the premises is also a large warehouse for reserve stocks, and another building near to the railway station is used for the storage of large quantities of agricultural feeding stuffs, meals, oil cake, etc. A well-equipped modern bakery also provides facilities for a large output of household, plain, fancy and Hovis bread, cakes, fancy buns and other pastry, all of which are made from the finest blended English and Hungarian flour under the most scrupulously cleanly hygienic conditions. In connection with the establishment is a circulating library well-stocked with a judiciously selected collection of works in every branch of literature which may be borrowed at a very moderate charge by subscribers. In this department may also be inspected a choice assortment of photographs, opalines, platinotypes, etc., including a popular speciality in Crossfield's Collotype View Books of Arnside and vicinity.

Consumers of the fragrant herb have for some years recognised a convenient source of supply from the well-selected stock.

Mrs. H. IDDON,

Private Lodging House,

Inglewood, ARNSIDE.

ALTHOUGH not so well known perhaps as neighbouring places, Arnside certainly possesses many points of attraction to the visitor, its convenient position on the Furness Railway, six miles from Carnforth junction rendering it a capital head-quarters for tourists desirous of exploring the charming and picturesque objects of interest in the Lake country. For this purpose "Inglewood," as Mrs. Iddon's establishment is known, will be found most central and convenient, the spacious house standing in its own well-kept gardens on the Promenade, over-looking beautiful Morecambe Bay, and commanding splendid views of the hills, and Grange on the eastern shore. The house is well-appointed throughout, the apartments being airy and commodious and the arrangements comprising every up-to-date convenience. Excellent cooking and good attendance is the rule, while the very reasonable charges in force, and the scrupulous cleanliness and well ordered management continue to render Inglewood an ideal establishment for visitors who appreciate the comforts of home-life amidst the most delightful surroundings.

FAIRY STEPS, NEAR ARNSIDE.

LEVENS HALL AND GARDENS.

LEVENS HALL AND GARDENS.

KENDAL AND ITS SURROUNDINGS.

K ENDAL is a picturesque and picturesquely-situated town in the county of Westmorland, on the right bank of the river Kent and distant about twenty-two miles from Appleby. It is a parliamentary as well as municipal borough, having had the distinction since the Parliamentary Reform Act of 1832. Agreeably blending antiquity with the most modern improvements and advantages, it is well worth the study of visiting tourists, and also admirably adapted for purposes of continued residence.

GENERAL VIEW OF KENDAL.

PAST AND PRESENT.

The proverbial mists that hang over most sublunary things, especially the origins of old English towns, are partly at least dispersed with regard to Kendal by the record of the settlement here of a number of Flemings under a certain John Kemp in the reign of Edward III. Their object was the manufacture of woollen cloth, and the "Letters of Protection" from the king named are dated in 1331. That the trade was soon a flourishing one is proved by a large number of historical and other references, the best-known of which, it is needless to say, is that of the valiant Sir John Falstaff, in Shakespeare's King Henry IV: "But, as the devil would have it, three mis-begotten knaves in *Kendal Green* came at my back, and let drive at me;— for it was so dark, Hal, that thou could'st not see thy hand,"

The madcap Prince's exposure of the knight's palpable lie is equally familiar; and Sir Walter Scott, in his "Lay of the Last Minstrel," makes reference to the prevailing colour of the garments, or rather the cloth, here manufactured:

> "Behind, in close array, and fast,
> The Kendal Archers, *all in green*—"

from which it appears that hue of the wares had become a common saying. "Kendal cottons," according to the quaint historian, Thomas Fuller, were also in his time—the seventeenth century—"famous all over England."

THINGS NEAR AND FAR.

Kendal Castle is among the former of these, standing on a considerable height at the east of the town. It was probably built by its first baron, Ivo de Talebois, who as already mentioned came over with the Norman Conqueror. At the present time it is little more than a fragment,

KENDAL CASTLE.

consisting of a moat, now growing some fine trees, a fairly perfect round tower, a keep, and a portion containing what is left of a round staircase. It underwent many changes of ownership, being for long in the hands of the Parr family; and here Catherine Parr, the last consort of Henry VIII., was born in 1513. The last member of the house, William Parr, Marquis o Northampton, took the part of Lady Jane Grey, and the castle is supposed to have bee destroyed in consequence.

Other interesting buildings are Sizergh Castle, about three miles south of Kendal, unlike the foregoing a well-preserved pile; Levens Hall, about five miles distant, on the Milnthorpe Road; Burneside Hall, about two miles to the north; Collin Field, a small and pleasant manor house; Cunswick Hall, Helsfell Hall, Abbot Hall, Black Hall, Brownsword House, and others, all not far distant, and well worth visiting. For the many charming walks, drives and excursions of the district, recourse must be had to the excellent local guides, as their number is too great for adequate treatment here.   Among the more notable places, however, are the Serpentine Walks, near by; *Scout Scar*, about two miles distant; Park Side, Hawes Bridge, the village of Natland, Bay Fell, Meal Bank, Benson Knott, Helm Fell, Boundary Bank, Ketel Well, the village of Burneside, and Levens Park.   The Race Course should also be visited.

Kendal, however, was doubtless of importance in Saxon times, Ivo de Talebois having been created first Baron of Kendal by William the Conqueror.   One of the descendants of the early barons, William Parr, was crested by Henry VIII. Lord Parr and Ross of Kendal, the bluff king marrying his eldest sister, Catherine Parr, as his last queen.

Many things happened in the ancient borough, which was incorporated by Queen Elizabeth in 1575.   There were plagues, royal visits in transit, military assemblies, and the passage and re-passage of armed men, Scotch and otherwise, and loyal or rebellious as regarded the reigning sovereign; so that its history was fully as picturesque as that of most English towns.

KENDAL PARISH CHURCH.

Modern Kendal is well built and of a pleasing appearance architecturally, being a happy blend of the old and new.   The two main streets are nearly parallel and run almost directly north and south, with various branch thoroughfares, chiefly at right angles thereto.   Its ancient connection with the woollen industry has been mentioned; but there are other manufactures, such as carpets (begun 1822), wool cards, leather (the noted *Closed Uppers*, especially), comb making, marble works, agricultural implement making, tobacco and snuff manufacturing, iron founding etc., and there are large paper mills in the neighbourhood.

RELIGIOUS BUILDINGS.

Kendal Parish Church is dedicated to the Holy Trinity, and stands very appropriately in Kirkland, in the southern part of the town.   As will be seen from our illustration, it is a structure of unusual interest and no little beauty.   The building is square, and has no fewer than five open aisles, the massive and commanding Norman tower being eighty feet high and twenty-five feet wide.   The Church, with the exception of the outer aisles, is supposed to date from the time of King John, a stone found near the Communion rails in a restoration in 1829 bearing the date, 1201.   Admirably restored, the interior has many features of great interest; the elaborate and effective roof, the excellent stained glass, the different chapels, and the many notable tombs and monuments, calling for particular mention.   The Parr chapel, at the end of the south aisle, has a few memorials yet remaining of the Parr family.   The Church is famed for its bells, which are ten in number, some of them dating from the seventeenth century, and also for the skill of the ringers.   The Register dates from 1555.

Other Churches of the Anglican body are St. Thomas', at the northern end of Stricklandgate, built, in the Early English style, in 1836; St. George's Church, on the eastern side of the river, near Stramongate Bridge, built in 1840; and All-Hallows Chapel, on the Fellside, dating from 1866.   There is a Roman Catholic Church (1836) in the New Road, the building being of hewn

ST. GEORGE'S CHURCH.

limestone and the style pleasing.   The Friends have a good Meeting House near by, and the Wesleyan and Primitive Methodists, the Presbyterians, the Congregationalists, Christian Brethren, Unitarians, and other denominations, have commodious places of worship in the town.

PUBLIC INSTITUTIONS, etc.

It is hardly necessary to say that the town is well provided for in all matters of public necessity and convenience.   The Town Hall is a fine building in Lowther Street, begun in 1825, and has a good clock tower, Council Chamber, etc., with a News Room and like accommodations. It contains a number of excellent paintings.   St. George's Hall, in Stramongate; Stramongate Hall, the Market Hall, Post Office, and the Banks, also are noticeable.   There is a good Free

Grammar School; the noted Sandes' Hospital School and Library, the Friends' School, and others, demanding mention as well. The Mechanics' Institute was opened in 1824, and is in every way excellent; and there are a number of good hospitals, charities, Friendly and other societies; more, indeed, than we have space to mention. The Corporation of Kendal is an able and public-spirited body, consisting of a Mayor, six Aldermen and eighteen Councillors.

TOWN HALL, KENDAL.

Kendal twice saw the Young Pretender's army in the rebellion of 1745—or at least a part of it. On the 22nd November, 1745, the first detachment of the Chevalier's army consisting of five of the Low-country regiments, with Elcho's life-guards, under Lord George Murray marched into Kendal. The next day the Prince followed with the Clan Regiments, the Duke of Perth's regiment bring up the rear guarding the guns. In this order they journeyed by Shap, Kendal, Lancaster, and Garstang to Preston where the regiments re-united. The Prince, who never spared himself, and voluntarily underwent all the hardships endured by the meanest soldier, journeyed for the most part on foot.   While crossing the desolate tract of waste between Penrith and Shap, he was so overcome by fatigue and want of sleep, that he found it necessary to take hold of one of the Clan Ogilvie by the shoulder-belt to prevent himself from falling ; and thus he walked several miles half asleep.   We can easily picture to ourselves the terror the northern army produced in the minds of the somewhat phlegmatic inhabitants of Kendal.   Stories had preceded their advent.   It is known to be a fact that many women hid their children under the impression that the Highlanders were cannibals, with a special fancy for roast baby.   There is a story told of Mr. Cameron of Locheil, the most chivalrous gentleman of any age.   One evening as he entered the lodgings assigned to him, his landlady, an old woman, threw herself at his feet, and with uplifted hands and tears in her eyes, supplicated him to take her life, but to spare her two little children.   He asked her if she was in her senses, and told her to explain herself ; when she answered that everybody said the Highlanders ate children, and made them their common food.

HIGHGATE.

Mr. Cameron having assured her that they would not injure either her or her little children, or any person whatever, she looked at him for some moments with an air of surprise, and then opened a press, calling with a loud voice : "Come out, children, the gentleman will not eat you." —(*Johnstone's Memoirs*).   It is notorious that no English person suffered harm to person or property by the rebellion of '45.

A second time Kendal saw the northern host—on its disastrous retreat from Derby.   The *Edinburgh Advertiser* gave in 1827 an account of a curious episode that took place in the town. The news of the retreat of the invading army had not reached Kendal, when on the market day, the Duke of Perth drove rapidly up the street, accompanied by an escort of horse.   The town and country people instantly took it into their heads that the rebels had been defeated, and at once resolved on capturing the Duke, in whose defence the escort fixed on the populace, many of whom had armed themselves with guns.   His Grace, putting his head out of the carriage window, with much timidity commanded his men to "fire high, it being useless to fire on a mob."   This thoughtless procedure was not unattended with loss of life, and gave rise to a circumstance involved in future mystery. The Duke's servant was knocked off his horse, upon which a countryman instantly leaped, and rode off. This was done in the heat of the rencontre, and no one had taken notice who the man was, nor was he ever discovered; on the horse was a portmanteau, containing a considerable sum of money. The servant died of his injuries, and was buried along with some others of his countrymen, in that part of the churchyard next the river; a flat stone, with a suitable inscription was laid down, commemorative to their fate.

Levens Hall in the vicinity of Kendal, is worthy of more than a passing notice. The original residence is said to have belonged at the time of the conquest to Tosti, Earl of Northumberland. Being escheat, it was given by the Conqueror to Roger de Poictou whose descendant sold it, *temp*. Hen II. to Norman de Redeman. From this latter family Levens was bought by the Bellinghams,

ABBOT HALL.

In the reign of James II. it was resold to Colonel James Graham, who dying without a male heir, devised it to Henry Bowes Howard who had married his daughter. It is now in the possession of Col. Bagot M.P. Interesting as the house is, its chief fame perhaps consists in its gardens. They are said, and we believe rightly so, to be the finest example of topiary in the Kingdom. They are laid out in the Dutch or old German style and are the work of Mr. Beaumont, gardener to James II. The walks and arbours are shaded by a profusion of yews, hollies, and other evergreens, cut into a variety of grotesque shapes and forms. The gardens are, we believe open to the public on Tuesdays, Thursdays and Saturdays, when the family is not in residence.

It was at Levens that Mrs. Humphry Ward wrote her novel "Helbeck of Bannisdale."

Sizergh Castle has been the home of the Stricklands for countless generations and is rich in architectural anquities and in carved oak furniture. It was at Sizergh that the antiquarian Thomas West, compiled his History of Furness which even in the present day takes premier place amongst topographical works in the district.

NETHER BRIDGE, KENDAL.

In the Parish Church there is a Strickland Chapel. A notable Epitaph in the said church is worth perusal it runs :—

"Here lyeth the body of Ralph Tyrer, late vicar of Kendal, B.D., who died June 4th., A.D. 1627.

London bred mee; Westminster fed mee;
Cambridge sped mee; My sister wed me;
Study taught mee; Living sought mee;
Learning brought mee; Kendal caught mee;
Labour pressed mee; Sickness distressed mee;
Death oppressed mee; The grave possessed me;
God first gave mee; Christ did save mee;
Earth did crave mee; And heaven would have mee."

HEVERSHAM, NEAR KENDAL.

KENDAL GRAMMAR SCHOOL.

Head-Master—The Rev. GEO. H. WILLIAMS, M.A.

ONE of the oldest educational establishments in the north of England, originally founded 1525: endowed by King Edward VI., 1548: and re-organised in 1886. Kendal Grammar School has since been greatly improved by the erection of new school buildings in 1889, and by the addition of a new school house in 1893. The new buildings, which provide accommodation for upwards of 120 boys, are erected on a site of four acres given by the late W. H. Wakefield, Esq., of Sedgwick. The site is an open one with a fine country prospect, just outside the town, and overlooks the river Kent. The new premises were opened in January 1889, by the Lord Mayor of London in state, assisted by the Lord Bishop of Carlisle, and comprise a large school, five class-rooms, library, physical and chemical laboratories, and all the modern equipment of a first-grade school. The school-house, which completes the beautiful block of school buildings, was finished in 1893. This provides accommodation for thirty boarders; the buildings are erected on

deep gravel soil, with south aspect for the dormitories. The scope of the foundation is to provide a thoroughly liberal and practical education: to prepare boys for the Universities and professions to the one hand, and for commercial life on the other. The school with all its advantages is open on all boys of good character and sufficient health, who are (i.) residing with their parents, guardians, or near relatives, or (ii.) boarding in an authorised Master's boarding house. An annual examination of the pupils is held in July by University Examiners, appointed by Governors and independent of the school. The fullest encouragement is given to all outdoor games in the excellent playing fields attached to the school, the cricket field (covering three acres) with pavilion, and an adjoining field of five acres reserved for football. The head master, the Rev. George H. Williams, M.A., late scholar of Jesus College, Oxford, formerly head master of Kingsbridge Grammar School, is assisted by a complete staff of masters fully qualified in all subjects included in the school curriculum. There are a large number of school and leaving scholarships. The school has been addressed on recent speech-days by the Lord Bishop of Carlisle, the Lord Bishop of Hereford, the Provost of Queen's College, Oxford, the Master of Trinity College, Cambridge, Sir John T. Hibbert, Archdeacon Diggle, Rev. Dr. J. Llewelyn Davies, and the Rev. Dr. John Watson ("Ian Maclaren"). Fees (Boarding and Tuition), £50 per annum. For illustrated Prospectus, etc., apply the Headmaster.

STRAMONGATE SCHOOL,

PRINCIPAL: MR. WILFRED SESSIONS, B.SC.

ONE of the oldest, as it is also amongst the most distinguished educational establishments in the north of England, is the Stramongate School, of which Mr. Sessions is principal, and in connection with which he has founded Dalton House as a boarding house for scholars, open to members of all denominations, recently extended to girls as well as boys.   The Schools may claim an unique distinction as one of the oldest in the Kingdom, having been founded in 1698 by the Society of Friends in Kendal, the present buildings having been erected in 1772.   Within more recent years,

CENTRAL BUILDINGS.   GYMNASIUM.

and under the direction of Mr. Sessions, the whole institution has been remodelled and enlarged, and furnished with the most modern appliances by the Board of Trustees to meet every requirement as a high-class educational and residential establishment.   Mr. Wilfred Sessions, B. Sc., the principal, is successor to a long line of distinguished educationists and scientists who have fulfilled the onerous responsibilities of head master of the schools as indicated in his qualifications as a Bachelor of Science of London University, Prizeman of Victoria University (Owen's College), Fellow of the Geological Society, and Fellow of the Chemical Society.   He had also, previous to his appointment to the Stramongate Schools had many years experience in two of the principal middle and upper class schools in the Kingdom, and has had exceptional opportunities of studying the educational system of Germany during his residence in Heidelberg where he acquired a practical acquaintance with the methods in use in that country.   The Stramongate school for girls, under the same trust, provides a boarding house for that section, most efficiently conducted by the Head Mistress, Miss Lucy Reynolds, B.A.   The school is recommended by a circle of very influential patrons, and a prospectus may be obtained on application to the Principal of the Stramongate Schools, Dalton House, Kendal, who will be happy to furnish full particulars as to terms, or arrange an interview with parents and guardians of prospective pupils.

Messrs. J. J. WILSON & Co.,
MANUFACTURERS OF KENDAL HORSE CLOTHING,
BELTS, BRACES, KNEE-CAPS, GIRTHS, &c.,
THE QUEEN KATHERINE WORKS, KENDAL.

THIS business was established in 1892 by Mr. John J. Wilson, a gentleman whose family have been connected with the woollen and leather trades for many generations.   Mr. Wilson has

A WORKROOM IN QUEEN KATHERINE WORKS.

not only had practical experience in all the departments of woollen manufacturing, but has studied the trade from the factor's point of view in some of our largest centres.

Queen Katherine Works are fitted with every appliance capable of producing good work, electric light generated on the premises being one of them.   The power employed in the works is supplied by a powerful engine of the newest description, whose absolute regularity is a guarantee of good work from the machines.   As set forth in our heading, the firm are manufacturers of the noted Kendal horse clothing, belts, braces, knee-caps, girths, and the like, together with all kinds of dog sheets, cow sheets, ankle boots, etc.   They do both a home and foreign trade, extending to America, South Africa, India, Australia, France, Germany, and other places, for which markets they have prepared most elaborate catalogues in over one dozen languages.   Recently considerable enlargements have taken place in the works, by which their facilities are much increased ; a jute and hemp sheet department has been added for the benefit of customers who are not purchasers of their higher grades of clothing.

The business is well organised, an especial feature being the provision made for the health and comfort of their employees.

TILBERTHWAITE GREEN SLATE CO.,

Head Office: KENDAL.

Quarries: Tilberthwaite, Coniston ; Kentmere, Staveley.

THERE are many green slates in the market, but for beauty of colour and durability none are to be compared with the beautiful sea green slates from the Tilberthwaite Quarries, Westmorland.

The geological position of these slates is in the Silurian or Upper Cambrian strata, and they contain as much as 78% of silica and alumina. Their colour is derived from the presence of ferrous oxide and magnesia. Some green slates, from their porousness, admit oxygen in such proportions as to allow the formation of ferric oxide, or the red oxide of iron, which causes them to discolour and decay. The Tilberthwaite slates, however, owing to their close texture, prevent this reaction, and retain permanently, in localities where the atmosphere is not charged with acids, their rich and beautiful green shade. The Westmorland green slate industry has of late years

VIEW IN ONE OF THE QUARRIES OF THE TILBERTHWAITE GREEN SLATE CO.

made wonderful progress in the way of development, by adopting the most recent and scientific methods in the production of the slate. The demand for the slates of the Tilberthwaite Green Slate Co. is ever on the increase, largely owing to the fact that they are now recognised as the most artistic and lasting cover for all kinds of public buildings and mansions.

The majority of the important public buildings in this country have been covered with slates from these quarries; amongst those covered or in progress we might mention the following :— New Municipal Buildings, Sheffield, opened by the Queen ; National Liberal Club, London ; New Roman Catholic Cathedral, Westminster ; New Admiralty Courts, London ; Royal Naval Barracks, Chatham ; New Victoria Law Courts, Birmingham, opened by the Prince of Wales ; New Technical Schools, Manchester ; New Post Office, Liverpool, etc., etc.

The Tilberthwaite quarries are situated in one of the prettiest valleys of the English Lake district, and are distant from Coniston station, on the Furness Railway, about four miles. The scenery all along the route embraces some of the finest and most picturesque in the district.

Messrs. E. RICHARDSON & Co.,

WESTMORLAND CHURN WORKS,

OLD SHAMBLES, HIGHGATE, KENDAL.

MANY noteworthy improvements in machinery and appliances in use in most up-to-date dairies trace their introduction to the above-named firm, who, since they were established in 1869, have won prominent recognition as manufacturers of churns, including gold and silver medal awards at the British Dairy Farmers' Association, the British Agricultural Society, and other of the principal exhibitions of the country. Messrs. Edmund Richardson & Co., have extensive premises in the Old Shambles, Highgate, Kendal, known as the "Westmorland Churn Works, Cooperage and Implement Depôt," which are fitted with all the requisite plant and labour-saving

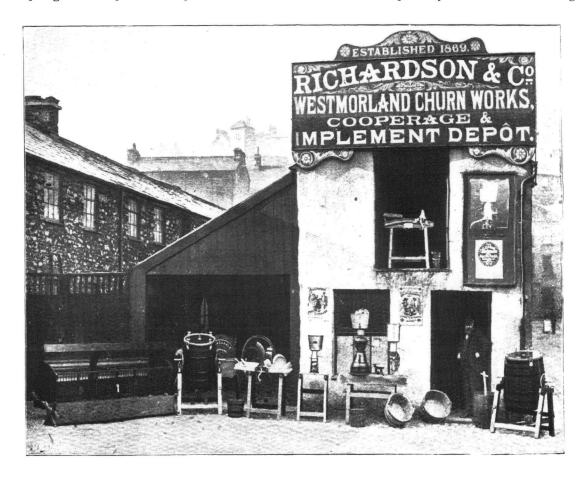

machinery for the manufacture of the firms specialities. These comprise their well-known and greatly approved "Princess" Churn, a marvellously simple and effective improvement on the old type of machine, easy to clean, having no beaters, and ensuring a more thorough separation of the milk from the butter, which is collected in globular form, accomplished by the peculiar shape of the interior. They are also manufacturers of the Royal Agricultural Society of England's Prize Barrel Churn, whose superiority over others was convincingly demonstrated by a First Prize award at the British Dairy Association's Show, held at the Agricultural Hall, London, 1881. Numerous testimonials and press opinions on the firms specialities in churns, etc., are embodied in an illustrated catalogue issued by them, which is obtainable on application together with prices and full descriptive particulars of their manufactures. E. R. & Co. would advise all intended purchasers of Dairy and Agricultural Machinery to write for price lists, and to inspect their large stocks before purchasing elsewhere.

OUR MOTTO :

. . . . Highest Quality of Goods at Lowest Prices. . . . .

Mr. J. H. HOGG,
Art Photographer, Dealer in Photographic Requisites,
71, Stricklandgate, KENDAL.

MR. HOGG has been associated with the development of photography since the year 1858, and has attained distinguished success in the practice of the art in the lines of landscape and portrait photographs, groups, etc. We may perhaps mention that he has obtained as many as eighteen prize medals for landscape and portrait work and the diploma of honour at Vienna (1891) for portraits, to which the following letters refer :—

VIENNA INTERNATIONAL PHOTOGRAPHIC ART EXHIBITION, 1891.

Mr. HOGG,   Vienna, May, 1891.

DEAR SIR,—We are pleased to inform you that pictures of yours have been accepted by the jury of artists.
As the former belong to the 600 chosen from among more than 4000, we think you will be gratified.
The Exhibition proves to be a great success, as there is not a single picture on the walls which has not artistic value.
Congratulating you on the success of your pictures, we are, yours faithfully,   CHARLES SRNA, President.
                                                                                        CHARLES ULRICH, Vice-President.

Vienna, June, 1891.

According to the rules of the International Photographic Art Exhibition each exhibitor is to get a diploma of merit, and the jury has the right to advise the patroness, H.I.H. the Archduchess Maria Theresa, to award a very limited number of gold medals. In consequence of this latter rule, this jury has subjected the whole exhibition to a careful examination. The result is, that it is found to be impossible, owing to the high merit of the pictures as a whole, and to the great equality of the several ones, to do justice by awarding medals, as of necessity some works must be passed by, which would not be justified, owing to their being so nearly equal to those winning medals. Therefore the jury has unanimously resolved that there shall not be double rewards, medals and diplomas. But each exhibitor will receive a diploma bearing the name of H.I.H. the Archduchess Maria Theresa, which, owing to the extreme rigour exercised in the selection of the pictures for exhibition, is, in itself, an honour of great value.   A. SCHAFFER, President of the Jury.
                                                                                        F. LUCKHARDT, Hon. Sec. of the Jury.

His studio and work rooms are centrally situated in Stricklandgate, Kendal, the arrangements being admirably suited for artistic execution in all branches of practice. The studio is in a separate building at the rear of the show rooms (which front on the street, as shown in our view), and is fitted up in the most scientific manner with regard to light, appliances, furniture, etc., while an excellent lawn is utilised for outdoor groups, and the like. All the usual branches of the art are followed, a special feature being carbon and platinotype work, and enlargements.

MESSRS. T. & E. RHODES,

WATCHMAKERS, JEWELLERS, OPTICIANS, GOLD AND SILVERSMITHS,

HIGHGATE, KENDAL.

WE give herewith a view of Messrs. T. & E. Rhodes' fine establishment, which, without question, holds the first position among concerns of its class in Kendal and district. The business dates from 1854, and is carried on in commodious premises in the main thoroughfare of

the town, near the Town Hall and all the principal interests. The window is one of the centres of attraction for all classes of the public, making a splendid show of artistic and elegant wares in the way of watches, jewellery, silver plate, and the like. Very large and superior stocks are held in all lines of the trade, including the best gold and silver watches, marble, gilt, and wooden clocks, time-pieces, etc., gold and gem jewellery of all descriptions, hall-marked gold bracelets, bangles, scarf pins, fancy dress rings, gold keeper rings, scarf rings, sleeve buttons, and so forth, silver and electro-plate forming an important department. The Messrs. Rhodes are noted for their excellent English lever watches, which have gained the highest reputation for durability and time-keeping qualities. Special value in presentation plate is one of the noted features of the house. Also fine leather goods, ebony brushes, mirrors, etc., and hall-marked silver-mounted small wares. Spoons, forks, cutlery, barometers, thermometers, spectacles and eye-glasses, fancy goods, brass work, etc., are also specialities. In all lines moderate prices rule. We may mention that the firm for the last thirty years have fired a gun at one o'clock p.m., Greenwich time.

Messrs. BAILIE & HARGREAVES,
Furnishing Ironmongers,
Central Buildings, KENDAL.

A complete assortment of articles of daily utility invites attention in the well-arranged

show-rooms of Messrs. Bailie and Hargreaves in Finkle Street, where they have always on hand a large and varied stock of furnishing ironmongery, comprising fire-side suites, fire brasses, curbs, fenders, trays, baths, fire irons, coal vases, travelling trunks and all the most improved types of wringers, mangles and other domestic appliances. The Central Buildings establishment presents also a tasteful display of Hink's duplex and 45 candle power round wick lamps, Rodgers' and Sons table cutlery, Britannia metal, nickel silver and electro-plated ware in elegant new designs. The firm are also sole agents for the "Encore" razors and keep in stock Bissell's carpet sweepers, the leading makers of register and other grates, tiled hearths, wood and iron chimney pieces, etc. Since the death of Mr. Bailie the partners are now the brothers G. R. & Samuel Hargreaves, assisted by Mr. G. R. Hargreaves jun. Both partners are deservedly popular, evidence of this good feeling having been recently exemplified in the action of the committee of the Working Men's Institute and the Excursion Committee, who presented Mr. G. R. Hargreaves with a beautiful epergne. B. & H. are agents for the celebrated "Herald" Kitchen Range, and the "Rex" specialities.

(Established 1854.)
Messrs. M. DEROME & SON,
AUCTIONEERS & VALUERS,
Chartered Accountants, Estate Agents, Stock and Share Brokers, Shipping Agents, etc.,
. . . 21, STRAMONGATE, KENDAL.

THE above firm, the members of which are Matthew De Rome, and Theodore De Rome, F.A.I., are experts in the valuation and sale of furniture, plate, pictures, books, old china, etc., and devote special attention to the letting and disposal of estates, residences and business premises. The disposal of landed estates has long formed one of the leading features of the business, and in the forty-four years or more during which the firm have been in existence, a very large volume of this class of property, including many of the principal residences in and near the Lake District, has been disposed of by them, while their services for valuations for probate, transfer, arbitrations, and the like, have been in constant demand. Some conception of the scope of the business may be gathered from the fact that up to the present time the firm have conducted as many as 2,860 sales, and have been engaged in over 5,000 appraisements and valuations. Mr. De Rome, Senr., is the oldest licensed auctioneer in the North of England, and his son, Mr. Theodore De Rome, is a Valuer to the Westmorland County Council under the Finance Act of 1894. The firm are the only Chartered Accountants in Westmorland.

H. BRAITHWAITE'S
. . Oriental Café,
30, Stramongate, KENDAL.

VISITORS to Kendal can ensure tastefully prepared and neatly served refreshments at the pretty and ornately decorated Oriental Café, conducted by Mr. H. Braithwaite, high-class confectioner and baker, whose business, established as far back as 1823, is one of the oldest in the district. The establishment has within recent times undergone considerable alterations and improvements, carried out in oriental style, and provides convenience in the well-appointed refreshment rooms, both on the ground and first floors, with lavatory and safe storage for cyclist's machines which are taken care of free of charge. All kinds of light refreshments with the accompaniment of delicious tea, coffee, chocolate and cocoa may be obtained at all hours, and a large reserve stock of plates, cups and saucers, teapots, trays, etc. as used in the Café and Japanese curios, are for sale if visitors desire to purchase them. Another speciality

meriting commendation is the Café tea and coffee, as served at the establishment. Other leading lines are bride and birthday cakes of richest quality. The Oriental Café is deservedly popular with tourists and cyclists visiting the neighbourhood, and is centrally and conveniently situated near the station.

ATKINSON & GRIFFIN,
PRACTICAL GUN & FISHING TACKLE MAKERS,
Sole Manufacturers of the Electric Cycle,

Telephone 0,249.   58, High Street, KENDAL.

OCCUPYING a prominent position near the Town Hall, this firm is the largest and best known of its kind in the district.

Manufacturers and patentees of Guns, Cycles, Fishing Tackle, Golf, etc., they enjoy a very high reputation for the excellency of their manufactures and to meet the demands of a large Sporting Clientele they handle a multifarious stock of requisites for indoor and outdoor sports; Cricket Bats, Lawn Tennis, Footballs, Fishing Coats and Waterproofs, Travelling Bags, Billiards, general sporting cutlery, electrical appliances, and mechanical toys. The Works are open daily for inspection where the manufacture is carried on by up-to-date machinery on economical lines and under practical supervision. Limited space does not permit us to do justice to this establishment, but tourists' would do well to visit this emporium where every information relating to sport in the district can be obtained.

Messrs. GREENWOOD & LITTLEWOOD,

TEA DEALERS, FAMILY GROCERS, & PROVISION MERCHANTS,

22, HIGHGATE, KENDAL.

Telephone No. 61.

ESTABLISHED in the year 1841, the above business is one of the best known of its kind in Kendal and district.   The premises occupied have a very striking and handsome appearance, the position being an excellent one in the main thoroughfare of the town.   The interior arrangements are commodious and well suited for the business.   Messrs. Greenwood and Littlewood maintain a large and well-selected stock in all departments of household groceries and provisions.   Teas are an important speciality, and are sold in packets suited for the popular requirements.   Coffees, also, with cocoas, flour, rice, sugar, tinned goods, pickles, preserves, sauces, spices, and other condiments, are extensively stocked.   Coffee grinding and roasting is carried on daily.

Provisions are fully represented, including the best classes of hams, bacon, cheese, butter, lard, eggs, etc.   The firm specially supply the high-class potted meats, soups, sauces, ox tongues, lobster, salmon, etc., of Messrs. Cunningham and De Fourier, and display a comprehensive assortment of the well known specialities of Messrs Lazenby, and Crosse and Blackwell; tinned fruits, bottled fruits, and high class jams and marmalades are also in evidence.   They have a large trade for yeast, the "D.C.L." brand for which they are agents, being very popular in the locality.   We may mention that the Senior partner Mr. Greenwood was the first tradesman to introduce the now old-fashioned German Yeast into the North of England, fifty years ago.

Mr. Littlewood is a member of the Town Council and Chairman of the Finance Committee.

Messrs. ATKINSON & SHARPE,
Ladies' and Gentlemen's Boot & Shoe Warehouse,
7, Stricklandgate, & 8, Finkle Street, KENDAL.

LIKE many other Kendal establishments, the business of Messrs. Atkinson and Sharpe is of good standing in point of age, having been founded about sixty years ago. The premises, of which we give an illustration, are conveniently situated at the corner of Stricklandgate and Finkle Street, several shops being connected together, and that in Finkle Street facing the Fish Market. The interior arrangements are commodious and suited for the trade carried on; the window display exceptionally tasty and attractive, an elegant and typical assortment of goods being exhibited. Very large and well-assorted stocks are held in all the usual lines of ladies', gentlemen's, and children's boots and shoes, the styles being distinctly fashionable and the materials of the best, while the prices are moderate in all departments. The firm are sole agents in the town for the noted " K " boots and shoes, and do a large business in these specialities. The Messrs. Atkinson and Sharpe's depôt is one of the well-known institutions of Kendal, and a well-established and thoroughly high-class connection is enjoyed in the town and throughout the district.

Mr. CLARENCE WEBB, F.R.H.S.,
Nurseryman, Seed Grower and Merchant,
Florist and Horticultural Sundriesman,
18, Highgate, KENDAL.
NURSERIES—STRICKLANDGATE, AYNAM ROAD, & TOWN VIEW.

DATING from the year 1810, when it was founded by " Meldrum," this business may correctly be styled " old established." In the hands of the present energetic proprietor it has been extended and developed to bring it thoroughly "up to date." The shop and sales department is in Highgate as above. Here an extensive seed business is carried on, noted particularly by many High Class and proprietory strains of vegetables and flowers also for certain strains of farm seeds. Seeds are despatched in the season from here to all parts of the Country, and also to the Colonies and America. The premises have an attractive frontage, rendered more so by the continually changing displays of nursery productions, pot plants, both flowering and foliage, together with up to date varieties of the choicest cut flowers. The bouquet and floral work generally is extensive and high class, the proprietor having on several occasions been patronised for Royalty, including H.M. the Queen. The nurseries are compact and are stocked with a good assortment of fruit and ornamental trees and shrubs. Herbaceous Plants, Border Carnations, and Cactus Dahlias, are specialities.

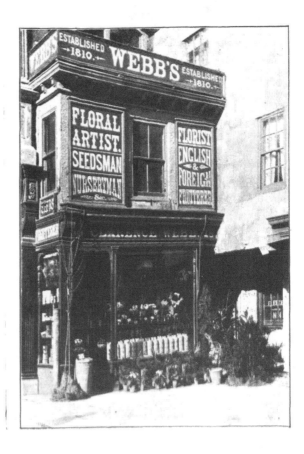

☙ MR. H. J. CROFT, ☙

CONTRACTOR TO
𝔥er 𝔐ajesty's 𝔊overnment.

TELEPHONE No. 59.
TELEGRAMS: "CROFT, KENDAL."

"Victory" Cycle Works,
Stramongate Bridge, KENDAL.

THE rapid development of the cycle industry is one of the striking features of the age, its more recent phase being the establishment of manufactories in many of the smaller towns as well as in the chief industrial centres. The first position in the district of which Kendal is the principal town is unquestionably held by Mr. H. J. Croft, whose premises, known as the Victory Cycle and Motor Works, are situated at the foot of Stramongate Bridge. The shop and show

rooms are very attractive, and make a fine display of machines and accessories, the electric light being used throughout the building. The factory is on the premises, and, in fact, the whole establishment was specially built and equipped for the trade and is in every way a model one. The machinery is of the most modern and perfect kind and is driven by a gas engine of eight horse-power, the electric light being developed on the premises and supplied to other business concerns in the neighbourhood. Excellent provision is made for every kind of repairs, which are promptly executed at moderate charges.

The Victory Cycle Works have been in operation for about seven years, and have gained a high reputation for their productions in the way of bicycles of a superior type. The various machines turned out by the works, comprising "Grand Victorys," "Victorys," "Popular Victorys," etc., have a distinct reputation, the first-named being an absolutely first grade machine, unsurpassed by any in the world, while the second is superior to most first grade machines of other makes. They are made of the best materials by skilled and competent workmen, and are guaranteed free from imperfections. We should mention also that Mr. Croft is agent for all the best makes of motor cars, of which a number are kept on hand for inspection.

Orders in all branches receive prompt attention and are executed with the utmost despatch. Price lists and full information are supplied on application. We should add that Mr. Croft is a Contractor to Her Majesty's Government, he having supplied the telegraph department of Kendal with cycles for the messengers.

KENDAL MERCURY, Established 1735, the Oldest Newspaper in Westmorland.) INCORPORATED
KENDAL TIMES, Established 1864, the First Penny Paper in Westmorland.)   1880.

Mr. EDWARD GILL,

Proprietor of the "Kendal Mercury and Times,"

Printer, Stationer, Bookseller, and News Agent,

11, FINKLE STREET, KENDAL.

Telegrams: "Mercury," Kendal.

We give a view herewith of Mr. Edward Gill's handsome premises in Finkle Street, Kendal, where a large variety of activities are carried on in connection with printing and the stationery and bookselling trade. The business dates from about thirty years ago and is one of the best-known in the district. The shop and sales department are very attractively fitted, and the windows make a typical and handsome display of stock. All the usual lines of stationery, with fancy articles of all kinds, books by standard authors, photographs, prints, engravings, etc., are well represented, and make a very pleasing sum total of wares, the goods being of a distinctly high class in all branches. A special feature of the business is the supply of novelties and Christmas goods, Christmas and New Year cards, private ornamented cards and mementoes, fancy calendars, booklets in great variety of design and colouring, children's toy books, standing figure reliefs, framed pictures, annuals, devotional books for presentation, including Bibles, Prayer Books, Hymnals, etc., and also the latest works by popular authors. He is also sole agent for Goss's heraldic ware, bearing the arms and seal of the County and Borough. The printing works are in the rear and are among the best-fitted in the country, two linotype machines being in use and all classes of printing done at moderate prices. As stated, Mr. Gill is the editor and proprietor of the Kendal Mercury and Times, the Mercury being the oldest and the leading County newspaper and advertising medium. The paper is set up and printed on the premises.

Messrs. MONKHOUSE & SON,

The Northern Counties Glass and China Warehouse,

60, HIGHGATE, KENDAL.

Telegrams: Monkhouse, Highgate, Kendal.   Telephone No. 245.

ONE of the largest and most comprehensive stocks of china and glassware in the North of England is to be seen at the above establishment, in Highgate, Kendal, of which Messrs. Monkhouse and Son are the proprietors. The business dates from about forty years ago, and has always held a leading position in the trade, the premises being in the principal commercial street of the town, facing the Town Hall, and admirably suited for the lines undertaken. As will be seen from our view, the frontage is double and makes an attractive display of goods. There are a number of well-arranged show rooms, three being upstairs, and several commodious warehouses, with packing sheds in the rear. It is quite beyond our purpose to enumerate the wares held, but generally speaking they may be said to include everything in the line of china, glass, and earthenware for public or private uses. One may inspect all kinds of cut and engraved glass; breakfast, tea, and dessert services; dinner services, and toilet sets of the latest designs, with attractive specialities in Continental ware from Dresden, Limoges, etc. All the standard lines are kept, from the English manufacturers including Doultons, Mintons, Copelands, and all the Staffordshire Potteries. An extensive wholesale and hotel trade is done, the resources of the house being shown by the fact that a stock of 5000 dozen tumblers are kept on hand as a regular thing. The connection in all branches is large, and orders are promptly executed.

Mr. WILLIAM HODGSON,

Ladies' and Gentlemen's Tailor,

"Specialite" Breeches Maker, Hatter, and Outfitter,

75, Highgate, KENDAL.

RESIDENTS of Kendal and neighbourhood, whether ladies or gentlemen, find it greatly to their advantage to obtain their supplies in the way of garments, and general outfitting articles at the above establishment, of which Mr. William Hodgson is the proprietor. The business dates from 1872, and has always been carried on on high-class lines, the patronage being of the best in the district. The premises are situated in the main thoroughfare of the town, in a central position, and are well suited for the class of trade done, the window being one of the attractive features of the street and always making an effective display of seasonable novelties. Mr. Hodgson keeps on hand all the newest and most fashionable materials for each season, comprising English, Scotch, and Irish Tweeds, Serges, Vicunas, etc., and a splendid stock of Harris and Bliss's Tweeds for shooting and riding breeches. All kinds of ladies' and gentlemen's tailoring is done on the premises, a skilled and experienced staff being employed. A leading specialty has always been riding breeches, this particular branch of sartorial wear being made by Mr. Hodgson for all parts of the United Kingdom and the Colonies. In all branches moderate prices are the rule, and a well-established connection is enjoyed throughout the district.

THE COUNTY MEWS,

Mr. A. H. Simpson, Proprietor,

Sandes Avenue, KENDAL.

THE County Mews, Kendal, were erected by Mr. A. H. Simpson, about six years ago, and to-day constitute one of the most perfectly equipped establishments in the North of England. The building is a stone structure of great solidity and handsome appearance. The yard measures 130 feet long by 30 feet wide, is covered throughout, and well lighted and ventilated, a large assortment of superior vehicles being at all times kept. Large chars-a-banc for pleasure parties, family omnibusses, carriages for balls and parties, landaus, victorias, broughams, waggonettes, dog carts and gigs, etc., with conveyances for funerals and weddings (a speciality), are always in readiness for letting. A stud of excellent and reliable hunters, hacks, and harness horses, are placed at the disposal of the patrons of the establishment, and competent and trustworthy drivers are furnished, coachmen in livery being supplied when required. There is first-class stabling accommodation consisting of over 60 stalls and boxes and the best arrangements for bait purposes, horses being taken in to keep by the week. Inspection of the premises is invited, and quotations made for all classes of work.

Messrs. E. & C. DAWSON,

Undertakers, Dress and Mantle Makers, Milliners, Cabinet Makers, Upholsterers and Furniture Removers.

WATERLOO HOUSE, KENDAL.

A somewhat unique but at the same time interesting combination of trades is carried on by the above firm in Kendal, the diverse nature of which is indicated by our heading. That, millinery, for instance, should be associated with cabinet making seems a little odd, but it is

explained by the firm's assertion that they aim to supply everything that a lady can put on her back or into her house. The Messrs. Dawson represent a business of long standing, the enterprise having been established so long ago as 1797 ; but although with a good century of business behind them they are distinctly up-to-date in all their methods and wholly abreast of the times. Waterloo House is centrally situated and well-adapted for the various lines undertaken. The premises are commodiously fitted, and a large assortment of wares is always maintained. The ground floor is devoted to the different branches of drapery, dresses, dress materials, and the like, with the usual accessories of the business ; while a handsome staircase leads to the show rooms for frocks, blouses, millinery, dressmaking, and mantles. The first floor is devoted to all kinds of furniture and upholstery, and the floor above to brass and other bedsteads, bedding, etc. The firm make a special feature of chimney pieces, cosy corners, wood bedsteads, sideboards, etc., which they manufacture extensively. Carpets are also a special line ; and, as set forth they are undertakers and furniture removers. The connection is large and extends throughout the district.

Messrs. R. W. & T. K. THOMPSON,

Hatters, Glovers, Hosiers, and Gentlemen's Mercers,
Boys, Youths and Men's Clothiers, Boys School Outfits a Speciality,

44, FINKLE STREET, & BRANTHWAITE BROW,

KENDAL.

A very wide range of fashionable and useful requisites is offered by the above firm at the address mentioned, the business having been established in another part of the town in the year 1876, and steadily developed on progressive lines since the start. The present premises, of which

we give a view, occupy an excellent corner position in the main thoroughfare from the Railway Station, near the Post Office. There is a large window frontage, and an attractive display is made in all the lines handled. The Messrs. Thompson, as set forth, are hatters, glovers, hosiers, and gentlemen's mercers, and also extensive dealers in juvenile clothing, Tweed and waterproof overcoats, umbrellas, travelling and hand bags and the like. Large stocks are maintained in all departments of up to date goods, and a number of important agencies held. The show rooms on the ground and first floors are well fitted and conveniently arranged, the assortment of goods being serviceable and excellent. Among specialities are Dent's gloves, Christie's and Lincoln Bennett's hats and caps, Morley's hosiery. In the rear of the premises are commodious ware-houses, where extensive stocks are stored, by which the firm are enabled to fill the largest orders at short notice. Moderate prices are the rule in all lines. The country trade is exceptionally large, and the connection is well established in every way. We should add that the firm are sole agents for the Cellular Clothing Co., Limited.

Messrs. VINCENT SMITH & FARRAR,

Dealers in Music and Musical Instruments,
Musical Agents, etc.,

15, STRICKLANDGATE, KENDAL.

Telephone No. 20.

WHETHER we are destined in no long time to become "a nation of singing birds" as was said of the country in the time of Queen Elizabeth, cannot be surely predicted, but it is certain

that the interest taken in music throughout the kingdom is widespread and yearly on the increase. The enterprise to which we devote this notice is an instance of the fact noted, having recently been established at the above address and already secured a share of the patronage of the music-loving public. The premises are centrally situated and well suited for the business, the sign of "The Fiddle and Hautboy" being a prominent and familiar object to residents and visitors. As shown in our view, an attractive window display is made in the various lines represented. The firm are experts in all matters connected with the trade, and keep on hand a large and well-selected stock of musical instruments, including pianos and organs by the best makers, strings and stringed instruments (of which they make a speciality), sheet and other music, and all the accessories of the business. The sole agency is held for Hooff and Co.'s well-known pianos, for which a good demand exists. Tuning, repairs, and the like are done by competent persons at low charges. Lessons are given on the violin, viola, cello, mandolin and banjo. The firm are in a position to supply any instrument at the shortest notice, and liberal terms for purchase are made. Agencies are also held for the Gramophone and the Edison-Bell phonograph.

Mr. WILLIAM LONGMIRE,

(Late C. & J. P. Gardner),

Coppersmith, Iron and Tinplate Worker, etc.,

38a, Stricklandgate (Opposite the Public Library),

KENDAL.

MR. WILLIAM LONGMIRE represents a business of long standing, the concern of which he is now the proprietor having been established in 1798. The premises are centrally situated in the main thoroughfare of the town, the windows displaying a typical assortment of wares in connection with the trade. A good show of stock is made in all branches of copper and tin articles, and also in culinary utensils, superior brushes, mats, etc. The workshops are in the rear of the premises and are supplied with all the usual appliances for the business, the tools and fixtures being of the most perfect kind. A good staff of experienced hands is employed, and all descriptions of coppersmith work, and iron and tin work, etc., are done at the shortest notice. A specialty is made of mill and factory work, which is promptly executed at moderate rates. Estimates are furnished on request for all classes of constructional or repair work, and workmen sent out any distance. All communications receive careful attention.

Messrs. JOHN FARRER & CO.,

Tea and Coffee Merchants,

Stricklandgate, KENDAL.

Telephone No. 20.

IN these days of stores and large emporiums representing half a score of businesses, it is somewhat unusual, and at the same time we must say a little refreshing, to find a concern devoting itself to one line of trade. This is the case with Messrs. John Farrer & Co., to whose old-established enterprise we have pleasure in devoting the present notice. Founded in the year 1836, the premises occupied are in the main commercial thoroughfare of the town, the frontage being of an old-fashioned type with bay windows, as shown in the illustration. The interior arrangements are in keeping, but well suited for the business carried on. The firm does an extensive wholesale and retail trade in their specialty, viz., teas and coffees of the best kinds, and are the only firm in the town doing the same class of business. Their facilities for obtaining the best grades of teas and coffees are exceptionally good, as they deal directly with the leading importers; and as their transactions are very large they are able to make terms highly favourable for themselves and their customers. Their various brands and classes of teas and coffees have gained a wide popularity in the district, and are in great demand with those appreciating the aromatic beverages and preferring genuine to spurious articles.

Mr. HENRY ROBERTS,

WHOLESALE AND RETAIL BOOKSELLER, STATIONER, AND MUSIC SELLER,

36, STRAMONGATE, KENDAL,

(And at Lancaster and Morecambe.)

A very wide and attractive range of articles and specialities of the above class may at all times be inspected at No. 36, Stramongate, Kendal, the business being old-established and of recognised standing in the town.   The premises are in the main street from the Railway Station, and, as will be noted from our illustration, present a handsome appearance, the window display being of exceptional interest.   A very large and excellent stock is kept in the usual lines of plain and fancy stationery, including commercial books, journals, ledgers, and the like, inks of all

kinds and the sundries of the trade, **a very large selection of standard books in FICTION, HISTORY, TRAVEL, BIOGRAPHY, Etc.,** by well-known authors, beside Bibles, Prayer Books, Hymnals, and other devotional works, and a large assortment of the best music, bound and in sheets.   A very attractive lot of fancy goods is also a feature of the business, comprising all descriptions of leather articles, work baskets, dressing cases, photographs and frames, photochromes, photogravures, etchings, and other works of art.   London parcels are had in daily, and magazines supplied to order.   All branches of bookbinding are also undertaken at moderate prices.   The business is both wholesale and retail and a large connection is enjoyed.

Mr. SAYERS HEAP,

GENERAL & FURNISHING IRONMONGER,

55, Finkle St., & 1, Kent St., KENDAL.

THE sign of the large gilt key is one of the familiar objects in Kendal, indicating as it does one of the most flourishing establishments in the district. Mr. Heap's business dates from 1842, and is carried on in commodious corner premises near the Post Office. As shown in our illustration, there is an excellent window display, especially in the way of brass and copper goods, the interior arrangements in all departments being well adapted for exhibiting goods also. As intimated, the stock includes all the usual branches of general and furnishing ironmongery, with builders' ironmongery, dairy utensils, and other specialities. The cellars are used for the storage of oils, nails, and general heavy goods. Both the ground floor and the upper floors are utilised for sale and show rooms, and a large assortment of articles is held in all lines. The

usual list of requisites in the way of cutlery, spoons and forks, culinary articles, joiners' tools and supplies, lamps, fire ranges, stoves, mantles, builders' hardware of all sorts, fenders and fire irons, brass and copper goods, bedsteads, mattresses, trunks, gardeners' requisites, etc., is very complete and of a superior class, the prices also being moderate and equitable. Agricultural implements are kept as well.

Mr. RAINFORTH HODGSON,

FANCY AND GENERAL BRUSH MANUFACTURER,

Dealer in Mops, Wash Leathers, Sponges, Baskets, &c.

Black Hall Brush Factory, KENDAL.

we cannot omit mention of the above enterprise, which is one of the oldest and best-known in the town. Established in 1838 by Messrs. Grant & Hodgson, Mr. Rainforth Hodgson became sole proprietor something over forty years ago, the business coming into the hands of its late proprietors, Messrs. Braithwaite & Tedcastle, in 1878. From the view given herewith of the premises it will be seen that the building is of the old-fashioned order—in fact, it is also an almost historic edifice, having been the residence of the first Mayor of Kendal, who ruled its civic destinies so long ago as 1575. But if the building is old, the machinery and appliances it contains are quite the reverse, and are fully up-to-date in all respects. And the same may be said of the working staff, and the methods on which the business is conducted. The Black Hall Brush Factory bears a wide and long established reputation for turning out the best and most serviceable kinds of wares, chiefly in the way of household, factory, toilet, and stable brushes of superior quality.

IN our attempt to give an adequate account of the various industries of Kendal and district,

Mr. THOMAS B. JACKSON, A.P.S.,

(Late Hind),

Family Chemist and Optician,

4, Stricklandgate, KENDAL.

We give herewith a view of the above premises, the shop being an old one with an attractive double front and the windows making a neat display of goods. The position is central and accessible, in the main thoroughfare from the Station and opposite the end of Finkle Street. Mr. Jackson keeps a well-selected stock of all the usual chemists' and druggists' supplies, including the best British and foreign drugs, etc., with a wide list of patent medicines and

proprietary specifics, surgical instruments, toilette and nursery articles, and the regular sundries of the trade. Dispensing also forms an important branch, Mr. Jackson being fully qualified as set forth above. Optical goods are stocked as well, the proprietor being a silver medalist in this department of his practice, and the greatest care is taken to adapt spectacles, eyeglasses, etc., to the sight of individuals. A special feature of the business is the supply of photographic appliances and accessories, all the best makes of apparatus being represented and a dark room provided for amateurs.

In connection with the photographic branch it should also be noted that Mr. Jackson has excellent facilities for developing and enlarging amateurs' plates and films, a convenience highly appreciated by votaries of the art residing or visiting in Kendal. As manufacturer of Jackson's Balsam Cough Syrup, the proprietor has introduced a very efficacious specific of well-proved value to sufferers from these complaints, its action being exceedingly rapid, giving relief in an hour. For laundry purposes warm commendation may be expressed of Jackson's "Easy" self glazing starch making starched goods like enamel in their surface finish. The business is conducted on the most equitable and efficient methods, and enjoys a high reputation for the excellent quality of its goods, and the skilful attention devoted to dispensing, etc.

Mr. JOSEPH PATRICK,

Retail and Family Boot and Shoe Maker, etc.,

"The Golden Boot,"

1, Entry Lane, KENDAL.

THE pleasantly situated Westmorland town of Kendal is no way behind others in its establishments for the common needs of the community, especially in the matter of boots and shoes. These essentials in a country so strongly inviting to pedestrian exercise are provided by a number of concerns, among which that indicated in our heading deserves prominent notice. The proprietor, Mr. Joseph Patrick, has not been in business quite so long as some of his rivals, but his eight years' experience of the trade has been highly profitable to him, if one may judge by the character of his establishment and the class of goods he keeps. The shop is in the chief commercial street of the town, near the Public Library, and has a neat and attractive double frontage and well-fitted interior, a workshop being in the rear. A particularly choice and up-to-date stock is held in all kinds of ladies', gentlemen's, and children's boots, shoes, and slippers, in black or brown leather, the qualities being of a superlative sort and offered at very moderate prices. The "J. P." waterproof shooting boots (warranted) are a speciality.

Mr. JOHN TYSON,

DRAPER AND MILLINER, &c.,

33, Finkle Street, KENDAL.

A VERY tasty display is made, and a particularly attractive stock held at the above establishment. The business dates from about seven years ago, and is carried on in commodious premises in a leading thoroughfare of the town, the position being convenient and accessible. The interior arrangements are well suited for the trade, and a large and very attractive stock held in all the usual lines of drapery, millinery, etc., including silks, dresses, mantles, jackets, costumes, trimmings, laces, ribbons, hosiery, gloves, umbrellas, corsets, under-clothing, and similar accessories. Household drapery of every description is one of the specialities of the business. Family mourning also receives great attention, and orders are filled with the utmost care and despatch. The agencies are held for the "C.B." and "H.S." corsets, and for Dent's gloves. The ground floor is devoted to general stock, the first floor to mantle and millinery show rooms, and the second floor to work rooms. A large and attentive staff is employed in the selling departments, as well as an experienced body of work-people, the business being thoroughly organised in all details.

Messrs. MASON & WILSON,

Cabinet Makers and Upholsterers,

"RED HOUSE," 37, HIGHGATE, KENDAL.

VISITORS to Kendal, and all persons desiring to furnish their houses either wholly or in part, would do well to call at the ware rooms of Messrs. Mason and Wilson, in Highgate, near the Town Hall. The premises, of which we give a view, have a spacious frontage and make a very attractive display of all descriptions of furniture and upholstery, several commodious show rooms being utilised. The selection is really of a distinctly high class, and notable for the artistic as

well as serviceable quality of the different articles. On the ground floor, three large apartments are devoted to the business, and an extensive assortment of well-made and handsome furniture exhibited. The stock includes all classes of drawing room, bedroom, and dining room suites, in a great variety of woods and materials, with hall and library necessaries, occasional chairs, tables, couches, and the like, in various artistic and pleasing styles. All kinds of mattresses, bedding, etc. (their own and by other makers), are also kept on hand, as well as a particularly extensive and choice assortment of wall papers. The upper floor is devoted to special drawing room and other suites, sideboards, wicker and other chairs, tables, and so forth. The firm supply every kind of carpet, oilcloth, linoleum, and like requisites for furnishing. An examination of separate articles and the prices thereto affixed shows that the system of moderate profits has been adopted by the house, and in fact bargains are to be had in all departments.

The cabinet works are situated on the opposite side of the street, and are equipped with all the most modern appliances of the trade, a staff of experienced hands being employed. The firm's facilities are of the best, and a steady and large connection is enjoyed.

Mr. R. Atkinson,

Bookseller and Stationer, Fancy Goods, Toys and Games,

1, STRAMONGATE & 2, KENT STREET,

KENDAL.

ONE of the most interesting depots for Fancy Goods and Stationery that we have ever had the pleasure of inspecting is that of Mr. R. Atkinson at the above address in Kendal. The premises of which we give a view, occupy a corner position in the main thoroughfare of the town

(from the Railway Station) and are literally crammed with stock, three rooms on the first floor as well as the entire ground floor being utilised for the business. Mr. Atkinson has a charming assortment, and an attempt to enumerate his goods would only end in bewilderment. The shop is *the* shop for presents, birthday and wedding gifts, toys and games of all kinds. A constant succession of new and taking articles fill its shelves, including pictures, framed texts, brackets, cupboards; Japanese and Chinese goods, trays, tea caddies, boxes, glove and handkerchief sets, mats, figures, curios, etc. Dressing cases, smokers' tables and cabinets. Fans in every style, novelties in lamp and candle shades. Benares brass goods, Eastern pearl inlaid coffee stools and tables, work boxes, writing desks, and toys and games of every imaginable kind. Children are greatly delighted with the department for horses and carts, farms, stables, soldiers, mechanical and steam engines, dissecting puzzle blocks, and the like. The line of English leather goods is particularly noteworthy, embracing all descriptions of ladies' and gentlemen's presents. A comparison of prices with those in other establishments of the kind shows that the scale is absolutely low, and in fact leads one to wonder how the things can be made for the money. It need hardly be said that the shop is well patronised by all classes, and always presents a very busy scene.

Visitors to the town and district during the summer months would find here a splendid stock of novelties suitable for presents for friends at home. Also views of the District, view books and many other interesting articles with views on.

Mr. GEORGE REISS,
WHOLESALE & RETAIL PORK BUTCHER,
15, Market Place, KENDAL.

ESTABLISHED about thirty years ago, and lately carried on by Messrs. Mogerley & Co., the above business is one of the best known in the district. The shop, of which we give a view, is centrally situated, near the Public Library, and accessible from all parts. The interior arrangements are of the most perfect description, comprising marble slabs and other conveniences for dealing with meat and keeping cool in hot weather. Mr. Reiss has had a wide experience in all matters connected with his business, and makes it a point to supply none but the best classes of pork in its various forms. He may always be depended on for excellent and appetising articles in the way of pork pies, cutlets, brawn, sausages (made by himself on the premises), hams, bacon, lard, etc., with the usual sundries of the trade. The establishment, which is the largest of its kind in the town, is a model of cleanliness and good arrangement, and large supplies are at all times kept on hand. Home-cured hams and bacons, home-rendered lard are specialities for which a large demand exists. The business, as noted, is largely wholesale as well as retail, and extends throughout the district.

THOMPSON'S
Glass and China Warehouse,
2 & 4, All Hallow's Lane, KENDAL.

ORIGINALLY established by the late Mr. Robert Thompson, father of the present proprietor, in 1839, the glass and china warehouse at the above address was taken over by his successor in March, 1899, who followed his sister in the management which has been in her hands for over twenty years. The premises in All Hallows' Lane, opposite the Town Hall, comprise a commodious building, with a double plate glass window frontage very tastefully arranged with a large and varied assortment of high-class ceramic ware of the leading potteries, and a large selection of glass in every form of utility and ornament in which it can be manipulated by the artistic craftsman. The building consists of three stories, with basement arranged as large stores, show and stock-rooms, in which are submitted numerous examples of artistic goods in dinner, dessert and tea services, toilet sets all in the latest and most attractive designs, while the items of the general stock will be found to embrace all table and decorative requisites, earthenware and kitchen and culinary articles in great variety.

HAYES & PARKINSON,

Carpenters, Joiners, Builders, and Undertakers,

Captain French Lane, KENDAL.

AN old-established and substantial business, originally founded many years ago by the late Samuel Compston, is now successfully carried on by his successors, Messrs. Hayes & Parkinson, both of whom possess thoroughly practical abilities as sound and experienced tradesmen in the above-named lines. The firm, who occupy a leading position in Kendal, have been entrusted with many of the principal contracts in the district, among the more recent being the whole of the joiners' work for the new Town Hall, Kendal. Estimates are submitted for the execution of carpenters' and joiners' work of every description, the erection of buildings on any scale, and the firm, as general undertakers, carry out interments in town or country complete in every detail at very reasonable charges. The premises in Captain French Lane, are commodious and well equipped with all the requisites for carrying out the work, in which an efficient staff are regularly employed. Messrs. Hayes & Parkinson enjoy a high reputation for the excellence of their workmanship, in all orders and contracts with which they are entrusted by their numerous customers.

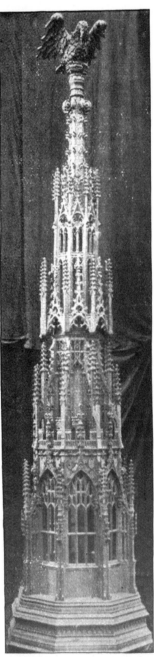

FONT COVER, KENDAL PARISH CHURCH.

Messrs. JOHN JORDAN & SONS,

BACON CURERS, CORN MERCHANTS, &c.,

The Granary, KENDAL.

THERE are certainly very few firms in the country who can claim a similar record for the superior quality of their English cured hams than Messrs. John Jordan & Sons, who have secured the principal prizes awarded for this class of home produce by the British Dairy Farmers' Association, in the years 1890, '91, '93, '94, '95, and '97, and who will doubtless maintain their reputation in this direction in future years. The firm is of very old-established standing, having been originally founded in

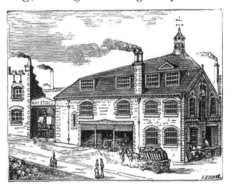

1836, and is still continued with steadily increasing success by the present representatives at the granary, and at the shop where the retail trade is carried on. The spacious premises in All Hallows lane, just off Highgate and opposite the Town Hall, are well arranged for the business, and provide the requisite accommodation for large stocks of hay, straw, corn, and other feeding stuffs, and agricultural requisites dealt in by the firm. They have also extensive curing houses, in which are provided all the necessary facilities for preparing the celebrated  hams and bacon, which form such a noteworthy speciality of their trade, and which, as suggested in the list of awards previously given, are regarded by the leading experts in the trade, are of quality unrivalled, both in delicious flavour and consistent excellence of condition. Messrs. Jordan & Sons are also agents for Samuelson's Prime Feed Cakes and Calf Meal, and are dealers in all kinds of artificial manures, basic slag and fertilizers, and feeding stuffs, which are supplied in accordance with the provision of the Act of 1893.

Mr. T. RATCLIFFE,

Dealer in Musical Instruments, Tuner, etc.,

Show Rooms, Sandes Avenue, KENDAL.

A well-selected assortment of high-class pianofortes, harmoniums and American organs may be inspected at the above establishment, where Mr. T. Ratcliffe has been engaged in this business for over twenty-five years, with constantly increasing success. The show-room, is centrally situated in Sandes Avenue, about five minutes distance from the station, and here are stored the latest models of pianofortes by Broadwood, Collard and Collard, Challen, Brinsmead, Ibach, Waldemar, and other eminent makers whose names are "familiar as household words" in musical circles. American organs are also fully represented in improved makes of Mason and Hamlin, Estey, Smith, etc. Instruments of best quality are supplied on the three years purchase system, the goods becoming the property of the hirer at the

expiration of that period. Mr. Ratcliffe being assisted by his son Mr. H. W. Ratcliffe, special personal attention and care are bestowed upon the tuning and repair o pianofortes, and their services are availabl

for the execution of orders in any part of town or country.

MILLER BRIDGE, KENDAL,

GRANGE-OVER-SANDS.

A MODERN village, though it is said to have derived its name from the fact that in ancient times the Canons of Cartmel Priory had a grange, or store-farm, for the corn grown in that part of their possessions. Its situation is singularly beautiful, and being sheltered from the north and east winds by hills, it has a climate that attracts to it visitors in winter as well as in summer. It contains a large number of well-built houses, many of which are boarding-houses or let out in lodgings. St. Paul's Church occupies a conspicuous position on a hill, and there are handsome places of worship also for the Wesleyans, the Congregationalists, and the Roman Catholics. Its salubrity, and the mildness of its climate, combined with the picturesqueness of its scenery, have rendered it one of the most

GRANGE HYDROPATHIC ESTABLISHMENT.

HAZELWOOD HYDROPATHIC ESTABLISHMENT.

favourite health resorts in the North of England. In the immediate vicinity to the railway station, what formerly was a piece of waste land has been tastefully laid out as a recreation ground, with pleasant walks and an ornamental sheet of water, surrounded by numerous shrubs and flowering plants. It has in its neighbourhood many charming walks and drives, and the views from the surrounding heights, such as those of Yewbarrow and Hampsfell, especially the latter, are magnificent. A couple of miles northward from Grange is a village called Lindale. Mrs. Gaskill resided here when she wrote her story called "The Sexton's Hero." The picturesque situation of Lindale Church cannot fail to attract the visitor's attention. Hampsfell is a limestone hill, distant about a mile and a half from Grange, and about 826 feet above the sea, crowned by a square tower, built by a

GRANGE OVERLOOKING MORECAMBE BAY.

former incumbent of Cartmel parish. It is called the "Hospice" and from the summit a splendid prospect opens out on all sides.   Mountain and valley, moor and fell, land

GRANGE ORNAMENTAL GROUNDS.

COTTAGE ON ROAD TO HAMPSFELL.

and sea, blend together in happy relationship, and present a grand panorama, to which no verbal description can do full justice.

HAMPSFELL HOSPICE,

Grange itself is somewhat of an "invalid's" place, a sort of northern Bournemouth ; but the hale and hearty, the sane in body or in mind, may find enjoyment in its vicinity.   It is a capital centre from which excursions may be made.   Cartmel, of which we speak later on may be visited easily from Grange.   The cyclist will find the place a Paradise.   The road may, if he extends his rides any distance indeed prove somewhat hilly, but the true lover of the art will appreciate the various gradients, they take away from the monotony of his ride.   An excellent day's excursion may be made by riding to Newby Bridge viâ Newton-in-Cartmel.   There is a steepish ascent after leaving Grange and then a most delightful run down to Newby Bridge, passing through or by Staveley.   Newby Bridge possesses a most excellent old-fashioned family Hotel in the "Swan," where refreshments may advantageously be taken.   A short detour will lead thence to Lake Side

GRANGE FROM THE NORTH.

station which is the starting point of the steamers on Windermere.   Or we would suggest that the "machine" be left at the "Swan," a boat chartered, and a leisurely row be indulged in as far as Lake Side.   These lower reaches of Windermere, which, one hesitates to describe as lake or river, are most delightful, reminding one of the most romantic portions of the Upper Thames. Mounting our iron steed again, we take the road from Newby Bridge to Haverthwaite and turning to the left run along Holker Mosses.   The way is one of delight, at places shaded by overhanging trees, at places skirted by the peat moss.   There is a scent of growing gale or bog-myrtle in the air, and the nutty savour of the flowering gorse.   There are the long white swathes of mist, creeping in fantastic patterns over the lowlands.   The hoarse crow of a cock pheasant from the Holker preserves breaks pleasantly on the ear.   And best of all, to the prosaic cyclist, the road is

YEWBARROW TERRACE, GRANGE.

ST. PAUL'S CHURCH, GRANGE.

perfection. At least it was when we last journeyed on it. Do not forget to pay a short visit to the new Church at Flookburgh as you pass, it will bear a close inspection. Do not omit to note the Cross in Flookburgh village, and if you be a man of inquiring mind, contrive to get into conversation with some of the Flookburgh Cocklers. They are most delightful folk, and will tell you a host of things you never knew before if you can only gain their confidence. Fancy a whole village living by the harvest of the sands! That is what these people do. They get their bread out of cockles with a few "fleaks" thrown in for make-weight. Everything here is regulated by the state of the tide,—concerts, balls, merry-makings, yes, even Church services, we believe, when these take place on a week night. If you want a new experience persuade one of these fishermen to take you "over-sands" in his cart next time he journeys to Ulverston. The passage

HUMPHREY HEAD.

over sands has its romantic element. There is a weirdness and sense of utter solitude and desolation when one is mid-way between bank and bank. The land on either side is dim and shadowy, unless the day be very fine; there are wide reaches of leaden sand; there are pools silvery or dark as they catch the light or no; there are white wreaths of sea-mist, salt laden and ghost-like, creeping up the channel. All these go to create an exciting experience. Once this over-sand route was the only means of reaching the towns in Low Furness, and many tales there be of misadventure, ay, and of death too, for ill fated travellers.

Another capital ride is from Grange to Levens Hall, famed for its gardens, which we have described elsewhere. The road is almost a dead level, but the country is somewhat bare and uninteresting save for its remote views. The journey may be prolonged to Kendal, and the train taken on the return.

YACHTS ON BAY AT GRANGE

GRANGE HOTEL.

Hazelwood Hydropathic Establishment,

Telegrams—
Hazelwood, Grange=over=Sands.

☙ GRANGE-OVER-SANDS.

MODERN medical scientists doing battle with that most insidious foe to health, pulmonary disease and allied affections, are now unanimous in their advocacy in recommending their patients to resort in the early autumn to various places on the English coast, which long experience has

demonstrated are best adapted as sanatoria for victims of the consumption scourge, and invalids needing a mild and equable climate. That Grange amply fulfils these conditions is expressed in the authoratative opinion of such eminent specialists as Dr. Walshe and Dr. Douglas Powell, both of whom strongly recommend the district, in their classical works on " Diseases of the Lungs," as a favourable winter and spring asylum for consumptive invalids. With the advantages thus briefly outlined, it must be conceded that Grange is an ideal health resort, and that no better site could be suggested for residential purposes than that occupied by the Hazelwood Hydropathic Establishment, formerly known as the Brown Robin Mansion, and converted to its present use in 1887. The establishment is built on the slope of a beautifully wooded hill on the north shore of Morecambe Bay, and is about seven minutes distant from Grange railway station, from which the house is approached by a turning to the right, leading by a picturesque road to the main entrance. It is about 100 feet above sea level, and stands in its own grounds of some thirty acres in extent, intersected by about two miles of footpaths, bordered by pines and other evergreens. The walks are not only well sheltered, but from many points command exquisite views of the Bay and the distant mountains of the Lake country and of Yorkshire. Ample facilities for out-door enjoyment are provided in the well-kept tennis and croquet lawns and concrete tennis courts. The house, which has been twice enlarged, now contains a dining room with seating accommodation for 130 guests, drawing room, smoking lounge, reading and billiard rooms, and a large recreation and ball room, with stage and fine grand pianoforte, wherein dances, private theatricals, and other entertainments are frequently held. There are about ninety bed rooms and private sitting rooms, many of spacious size, and the various corridors are exceptionally wide and airy. The sanitorium heating and lighting are designed throughout on the most recent principles. The establishment is well appointed, replete with every comfort, and an equable temperature of about 56 to 60 degrees day and night throughout the winter. The medical depart-

ment is under the direction of Richard Lowther, M.D., M.R.C.S., and Owen Gwatkin, M.R.C., L.S.A., but all enquiries should be addressed to the Manager. The terms are most moderate, being from £2 12s. 6d. from October 1st to June 30th, and from £2 2s. from July 1st to September 30th, according to situation of bed room. Medical attendance and special baths are extra.

RIGG'S HOTEL,

GRANGE-OVER-SANDS.

... A SUMMER AND WINTER RESIDENCE.

THIS Hotel, delightfully situated on the shores of Morecambe Bay, is in the direct route to the Lake District, being only eight miles from the foot of Windermere Lake, and communicating by rail with Furness Abbey, Coniston, Wastwater, &c. The train service is excellent from all parts, and passengers can arrive by Midland or North-Western Rails by through trains from London, St. Pancras or Euston stations, in 6½ hours; Liverpool, 2½ hours; Manchester, 2¼ hours; Preston, 60 minutes; Leeds and Bradford, 2 hours; Windermere, Lake Side, 30 minutes. All trains stop at Grange-over-Sands. Grange is on the limestone formation, and the neighbourhood abounds in beautiful walks and drives. The Hotel being well sheltered by hills on the north and east, is admirably adapted for a winter residence or for invalids, the climate being similar to that of Torquay or Devonshire. The water supply is exceptionally good and plentiful, being brought from Newton Heights, five miles from Grange, and is the purest supply in the neighbourhood. Medical officer's analysis may be had on application.

Lawn Tennis. . Good Golf Links.

ESTABLISHED 1789.

COWARD'S CROWN HOTEL,

GRANGE-OVER-SANDS.

Proprietor: Mr. John Coward.

Easy reach of Golf Links.   Telegrams: Crown, Grange.
Bus meets all trains.   Headquarters C.T.C.

hospitality to generations of visitors and tourists in search of health and pleasure on the banks of Morecambe Bay, which is acknowledged as among the most delightful holiday resorts on the British coast. The establishment is situated on an eminence at the end of Main Street, commanding beautiful views of the surrounding mountain scenery and is replete with every comfort and convenience of a modern hotel. Excellent cooking and efficient service are the rule, and a well varied and tempting menu is daily submitted for luncheons and dinners in the public room. The hotel is noted for the excellence of its wines and spirits, special attention being devoted to this department by the proprietor, by whom family orders are also supplied. Attached to the establishment are stabling, coach houses, etc., for a number of conveyances, opened and closed carriages, all well-horsed and in charge of trustworthy drivers which may be hired at reasonable charges for drives and excursions to the numerous places of interest,

ONE of the oldest hotels in the district, "The Crown" has for a century offered historical and romantic, in the charming district surrounding Grange.

DENTS' PRIVATE HOTEL,
THE ESPLANADE,
GRANGE-OVER-SANDS.

THE MISSES DENT are to be congratulated upon the very excellent arrangements they have provided for the comfort and convenience of visitors to this popular holiday resort, where their well-known private hotel and family boarding house has been established about four years. The house is charmingly situated on the Esplanade, over-looking Morecambe Bay, commanding beautiful and diversified views of the surrounding sea and landscape on all sides. It is conveniently located within five minutes walk of the railway station, landing stage, church, post office, and near the Golf Links, while within the immediate vicinity are numerous lovely walks, drives and excellent boating and bathing grounds. The establishment is furnished and arranged throughout in the most up-to-date style, the accommodation including handsomely appointed coffee and smoking rooms, private apartments en suite, and a number of airy and comfortable bed rooms provided with hot or cold baths, lavatories, etc., on each landing, the entire arrangements being well-ordered and complete in every detail for the convenience of visitors. Good cooking and attentive service are other marked features of the Misses Dents' management. These ladies are unremitting in their efforts to ensure the enjoyment of their guests.

Mr. GEORGE WARBURTON,
PRACTICAL BOOT AND SHOE MAKER,
GRANGE-OVER-SANDS.

THE best quality of material, skilful workmanship and superior finish are always assured in the class of goods supplied by the well-known tradesman above-named, who has been established in business here since 1867, and worthily enjoys the liberal support of the local gentry, and residents and visitors in the neighbourhood, who have become aware by long experience that every article of his make is thoroughly reliable and durable in wear. At the neatly-appointed shop, Mr. Warburton has always in hand an excellent assortment of boots and shoes for ladies' and gentlemen's ordinary and dress and evening wear specimens of which in all the latest styles may be inspected in the window, where an attractive show of goods is on view. Special lines of the business are the execution of bespoke orders for gentlemen's walking, shooting or riding boots, ladies' boots and shoes in any style or children's wear, for which lasts are specially fitted if required. Only thoroughly experienced hands are employed in making up, and in connection with this branch repairs are

neatly and promptly carried out at exceedingly reasonable charges, and sent home the same day when desired.

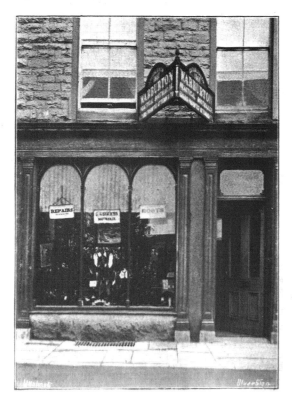

Mr. A. W. HANKINSON,

DISPENSING AND FAMILY CHEMIST,

Grange=over=Sands.

INVALIDS and patients under medical treatment resorting to this district, will find every facility for obtaining the remedies prescribed by their professional attendants at the above establishment, where careful attention is bestowed upon the preparation of physicians' prescriptions and family recipes by the proprietor, a fully qualified and skilful dispenser. Mr. Hankinson has always in stock the necessary drugs, etc. for this purpose, together with patent and proprietary articles, perfumery, toilet and nursery requisites, and surgical and medical appliances of every description. He also supplies photographic apparatus and accessories, and for the convenience of the numerous amateur photographers who frequent the neighbourhood, a capital dark room has been arranged for the development of negatives. The developing and printing of customers' negatives are undertaken if desired, at reasonable prices. The premises have an attractive window frontage and roomy interior accommodation on the ground floor with

photographic show-room above, extensive alterations having recently been made, with the object of bringing the business up-to-date. There is also a well-stocked circulating library, replete with some hundreds of works by the standard authors and most popular writers of the day, which are obtainable on very moderate terms of subscription by residents and visitors in the locality. A large and varied stock of Photographs and Photographic Albums of the vicinity and of the Lake District, by Valentine and Sons, and Frith and Sons is kept. Aërated and

Mineral Water of the first quality can be obtained in Syphons and Bottles.

Mr. S. BROADBENT,

FISH, GAME AND POULTRY DEALER,
ENGLISH and FOREIGN FRUITERER,
MAIN STREET,
GRANGE-OVER-SANDS.

The choicest qualities of fish, game and poultry in season are always to be obtained at Mr. Broadbent's well-known stores opposite the Post office in Main Street, where an extensive trade is carried on in these branches. The premises have an attractive double window frontage to the leading thoroughfare of the town, and are neatly appointed in modern style, presenting at all times a scrupulously cleanly appearance, indicating the care bestowed on this detail of the arrangement. Fresh supplies are daily to hand of all kinds of fish, game and poultry which are purveyed in prime condition for the table, and on one side is a tempting display of delicious English and foreign fruit of the choicest quality the season produces. Mr. Broadbent also holds a large stock of the purest Wenham Lake ice, and is also noted for the excellence of the oysters and shell fish he supplies. An extensive connection among private families hotels, boarding houses, etc., is served in all parts of town and th country, where orders are promptl and punctually delivered.

Mrs. HARRISON,

Needlework and Fancy Repository,
Yewbarrow Terrace, GRANGE-OVER-SANDS.

A most attractive and prettily-arranged display of artistic and tasteful goods is always on view in the handsome plate glass window of Mrs. Harrison's establishment which was opened as a needlework and fancy repository by this lady some six years ago on her removal from Bowness, where she had previously been in business for 20 years. The premises, situated in Yewbarrow Terrace, have a neat single window frontage, and are fully stocked with all the ladies' fancy work offering a wide selection of these requisites in all current shades and colours. The residential portion of the establishment has been adapted as private furnished apartments for visitors, for which a separate entrance is available next to the shop. There are seven well furnished sitting-rooms and bed-rooms, provided with bath-room—hot and cold water service—and every comfort and convenience for tourists or families staying in the house. The apartments command beautiful views of Silverdale, the lake and ornamental grounds, are situated close to the railway station, and may be commended to visitors as combining all the comforts of home life amid the most delightful surroundings.

Mrs. PERCIVAL BLYTH,

GENERAL DRAPER, MILLINER, GLOVER, & HOSIER,

Main Street, GRANGE=OVER=SANDS.

VISITORS to this delightful health resort will experience no more difficulty in obtaining their shopping requirements at the above establishment than they would in the metropolis or large provincial centres, Mrs. Blyth being invariably up-to-date with an attractive display of the latest

novelties and styles in all the items of a lady's fashionable toilette for either indoor or outdoor wear according to the demands of the current season. The handsome corner shop in Main Street is one of the features of the thoroughfare, the plate glass windows being effectively arranged with a tasteful assortment of goods in all the principal lines represented in the large and specially selected stock while the interior is equally well adapted for the sale departments. The general drapery department shows a varied stock of dress goods, household linens, lace curtains and similar furnishings, all of the first quality of manufacture, and an immense assortment of fancy goods, gloves, hosiery, offer a wide variety for choice, and artistic needlework is admirably epresented; also articles of different kinds for presents. Thompson's "D.C.B." Corsets, also ther popular makes. Agents for P. & P. Campbell's Dye Works. In addition to an extensive onnection among residents and visitors in the locality, the business enjoys substantial support om numerous customers in all parts of the country whose orders are executed through the post. isitors to Grange would do well to call at the address and inspect the various wares offered.

J. W. JOPSON, & SON,
Family Grocers and Tea Dealers, Bakers and Confectioners,
GRANGE-OVER-SANDS.

FIRST-CLASS quality of purveying is made a speciality by Messrs. Jopson & Son, who since 1864, has successfully cultivated a progressive trade in this line (Mr. Jopson junr. was taken into partnership in 1899), which now claims the substantial support of a numerous connection in the town and district. The well-arranged shop with its double-window frontage is a familiar feature of the leading thoroughfare and is fully stocked with the choicest and most popular blends of family teas, fresh ground coffee, the primest Wiltshire mild-cured hams and bacon and all the best known brand of home, foreign and colonial produce in high-class provisions. On the premises, the firm have had specially constructed an excellent bakery with patent steam oven in which is made the purest and most nourishing plain and fancy household bread, cakes, biscuits and pastry, which are supplied to customers at their own residences who are waited upon daily for orders. In 1899 they were awarded a certificate for making household bread, the competition was an open one, and there were about one hundred competitors.

Mr. H. E. ROBINSON,
Watchmaker, Jeweller and Optician,
Main Street, GRANGE-OVER-SANDS.

AN exceptionally attractive display of pretty novelties and elegant and useful articles is quite a feature of this establishment, the only one of the kind in town, and widely known in the locality for the excellence and variety of the goods supplied. Mr. Robinson, who has had the business for some years, is a thoroughly practical master of the watchmaker's and jeweller's arts, and has always on hand a large stock of the best makes of English and imported goods in these lines, together with a capital selection of sterling silver and electro-plated ware, spectacles, folders and glasses to suit all sights, field, opera and marine glasses, and a choice assortment of specialities in aluminium metal such as card cases, match boxes, ash trays, and other articles suitable for birthday and wedding gifts, souvenirs, etc. Careful attention is given to the repairs of all kinds of jewellery, watches, clocks and intricate mechanism, which is executed in workmanlike style with skill and despatch. Mr. Robinson also undertakes the winding and adjustment of public or private clocks by the month or year, this duty being entrusted only to thoroughly reliable hands.

ESTABLISHED 1861.

Messrs. W. & J. MOSSOP,

Grocers and Provision Merchants, Millers, Bakers and Confectioners,

GRANGE=OVER=SANDS.

Corn Mill:—LINDALE-IN-CARTMEL.

ESTABLISHED in 1861, the above concern has had an increasingly prosperous career, and now holds a recognised position.   The premises which are spacious and well appointed are situated

near the Crown Hotel, and the firm are noted for the reliable excellence of each class of goods and produce supplied.   The shop has a fine double frontage, and makes an attractive display in all the usual lines of groceries and provisions, with the customary accessories.

The interior is spacious and well fitted in every way, and a large stock is always maintained in all the various articles of the trade.   Our readers may judge the character of the business when we mention that the well-organised departments embrace, teas, coffees, cocoas and chocolates, general groceries, fruits and confectionery, provisions, bakery and milling which enables the firm to prepare meal and other food stuffs at their Lindale Mill. The lines in all departments are exceptionally full, and an inspection of the stock shows it thoroughly sound and of excellent character.

On the premises also is a well-equipped bakery for the production of plain and fancy household bread, bride and birthday cakes which are made on the shortest notice with artistic decorations in icing and piping.   A visit shows at once the carefully-elaborated arrangements to ensure cleanliness, purity of ingredients, and scientific methods of compounding and baking. The ovens and appliances are strictly modern, and all the more recent and approved inventions are made use of.

Great care, too, is taken in the handling of the goods after baking, so that they may be in the best condition.   It should be noted that in 1898 the firm was awarded by "The Master Bakers and Confectioners Society"—a Gold Medal and two Diplomas for excellence and purity in baking bread in open competition.

Messrs. Mossop's Digestive Brown Bread, prepared from the finest wheat by their own process, and as evidenced by the analytical reports open to inspection, unrivalled for dietetic purposes.   Also bakers of the celebrated Hovis Bread.

The firm are agents for Mazawattee Teas, and have also a high reputation for the freshness of their coffees which are ground daily on the premises.

KENTS BANK.

MAY be properly described as a continuation of Grange. It is noticeable as having been, before the construction of the railway, the point of starting and returning across the sands between Ulverston and Lancaster. And the records of the district abound with sad accounts of persons who were drowned while attempting to cross the sands without a guide. The principal guide was named Carter, and the office had been held by his ancestors for many generations. On leaving Kents Bank, Allithwaite, with its church and schools is seen on the top of a hill on the right. Here the railway crosses

KENTS BANK.

a promontory called Humphrey Head, from the summit of which a grand view is obtained of Morecambe Bay and the shore enclosing it. Kirkhead Cave is on the south side of a hill between Kents Bank and Humphrey Head. The entrance to the cavern is 4½ feet high, and within the roof rises to a height of from 18 ft. to 20 ft. high. A considerable number of pre-historic remains, such as bones—human and animal, fragments of pottery, and bronze implements were found there. Near the base of Humphrey Head is "Holywell Spa," a medicinal spring, which is said to be efficacious for the cure of gout, and bilious and rheumatic disorders. Its properties resemble the salt spring of Kissengen in Bavaria and Wiesbaden in Nassau. Those who wish to make trial of its virtues can obtain the key at Wyke Farm close by.

ABBOT HALL PREPARATORY SCHOOL,

KENTS BANK, GRANGE=OVER=SANDS.

Head Master   -   -   Mr. HUBERT LOWRY, M.A.

SITUATED in one of the most healthy places on the English coast, the Abbot Hall Preparatory School occupies an exceptionally advantageous position for a training centre for boys between the ages of eight and fifteen, undergoing the preliminary stages of a high-class education previous to entrance in our great Public Schools with an ultimate view to a University career. The school is under the personal direction of Mr. Hubert Lowry, M.A., Hertford College, Oxford, and formerly Captain of Westminster School, assisted by a resident master (graduate in Honours) whose tuition

is also supplemented by that of visiting masters thoroughly proficient in each branch of instrumental music undertaken by the pupils. Abbot Hall is at Kent's Bank on the Furness Line, half-an-hour's journey from Carnforth Junction on the L. & N.W. and Midland Railways, the large and commodious house standing in its own grounds having a south aspect, well-sheltered from the north and east and close to the sea, peculiarly suited for delicate boys. The building is of modern arrangement in every detail of sanitation and ventilation, and contains light and spacious school-rooms, dining-hall, dormitories and all the conveniences for residential purposes. The grounds cover an area of about twelve acres in extent, and include a large field for cricket, football, and other out-door games, which are played regularly under the supervision of a master. The boys are thoroughly grounded in the subjects required by the Public Schools, viz: Classics, Mathematics, English and French, those in the higher forms learning Greek, unless it has been decided that they are to enter the "Modern Side" of a Public School. The health and general comfort of the boys receive the closest personal attention of Mrs. Lowry, who is assisted in these duties by a competent matron who bestow special care in the case of delicate boys. Full particulars as to terms, etc., may be obtained from the Head Master on application, and with these are also included the names of highly influential noblemen including His Grace the Duke of Buccleuch, K.G., the Right Hon. the Viscount Cross, G.C.B., and numerous clergymen and gentlemen by whom the School is recommended or who have been parents of past and present pupils.

CARK AND HOLKER.

CARK contains a noticeable mansion called Cark Hall, an old manor house, the ancient seat of the Curwens. This house still preserves some features of interest, but it has been considerably altered and modernised, and has been converted into two dwellings. Flookburgh is a fishing village, noted for its flounders and cockles, lying at a distance of about three quarters of a mile from Cark. It was anciently a market town, a charter having been granted to it by Edward I. A maltese cross standing in the village bears on its base the following inscription :--First Charter granted to Flookburgh by Edward I., A.D. 1278, Second Charter granted by Henry IV. A.D. 1412. Charter confirmed by Charles II. A.D. 1675. Erected A.D. 1882, on the site of an ancient cross. The Charter of Edward I. permitted the prior of Cartmel to hold a market at Flook-burgh on certain days in the year. Henry IV. granted permission to his son the Duke of Clarence to hold a market there every Tuesday and two fairs yearly. This charter was confirmed by Charles II., but in the latter part of his reign was included in a general order tha corporate towns should surrender their charters, in order that they might be granted afresh The church, dedicated to St. Mary, is a plain stone edifice rebuilt in 1778. A new church is at present (1900) in course of erection on a different site.

HOLKER HALL.

Holker is a village, distant about half a mile from Cark station. Holker Hall was the favourite seat of the late Duke of Devonshire, and it was here that he spent the last days of his life. It is now the property of his grandson, the Hon. Victor C. W. Cavendish. The park by which it is surrounded has an extent of more than 200 acres; it stretches down to the shore, and contains trees of great size and beauty. The mansion contains among other objects of interest, some finely carved oak furniture, and also a collection of pictures; The gardens which surround the Hall, contain some fine conservatories filled with choice flowers and plants, these together with the majestic forest trees and flowering shrubs, cannot fail to excite the admiration of visitors.

CARTMEL.

THE old fashioned town of Cartmel is about 2½ miles from Cark station. It is situated in a fertile valley, through which run two streams, one flowing north and the other south. It was between these two streams, that the Priory was erected in 1188, for canons regular of the order of St. Augustine, by William Mareschal, Earl of Pembroke. At the dissolution of the monasteries the priory church, though partially unroofed, was saved from destruction in consequence of its being used also as a parish church. But 80 years passed and it was fast hastening to decay, when George Preston, Esq., of Holker, undertook to repair it. It was then that the elaborate screen work was placed round the choir, and

CARTMEL PRIORY CHURCH.

though the church has since then passed through a period of neglect, much has been done during the last 50 years to restore it as far as possible to its ancient grandeur. It is cruciform in shape, and the length of the church is 160 feet, the transepts 110 feet, the width of choir and aisles 76 feet, length of choir 61 feet, width of nave and aisles 65 feet, length of nave 71 feet, and height of tower 71 feet. The galleries which once disfigured it have been removed, the whitewash taken off from the pillars, walls and arches, and open benches of oak have been substituted for the unsightly square pews. The centre is supported by four finely clustered pillars, and a triforium arcade runs round the chancel. It contains some interesting monuments; one very remarkable monument is to the memory of Sir John Harrington and his wife; and there are several stained glass windows, principally modern. The east window, which contains a few relics of ancient glass, was inserted in the 15th century. It is 45 feet high by 24 feet in breadth. The reredos is of painted oak, the panels being decorated with the figures of our Lord and His Apostles. It was the work of Lady Louisa Egerton. The most noticeable external feature of this church is the diagonal belfry on the central tower. It is believed that no similar instance is to be found in any church in England. In the vestry there is a valuable library comprising about 300 books, chiefly of divinity. An ancient umbrella, supposed to be more than 200 years old, is also preserved here. The only relic of the monastic buildings, apart from the church, is the ancient arched gateway, which stands on the north side of the Market Square.

Soon after the train leaves Cark station a glimpse on the right is obtained of Holker Hall, and soon after another iron bridge is crossed, built across the estuary of the Leven, the river which flows out of Windermere. When the estuary is crossed the train reaches Plumpton Junction,

INTERIOR CARTMEL PRIORY CHURCH.

when on the right a branch line diverges to Windermere Lake. This line is described in Circular Tour No. 20 (see back page of cover). As the train approaches Ulverston, a monument built to resemble the Eddystone lighthouse, will be conspicuous on a hill, called Hoad Hill, on the right. The monument, which is 100 feet in height, was erected in 1850 to the memory of Sir John Barrow, Bart., who was born of humble parentage in a cottage at Dragley Beck, and by means of his persevering energy obtained a position of great eminence and wealth. He was a distinguished traveller, and for many years was a Secretary of the Admiralty. He was also a prolific writer, and the author of many valuable works on travel and other subjects. The tower may be ascended and from the summit a most magnificent panorama is to be obtained, scarcely to be surpassed in any part of England.

ULVERSTON.

(Passengers change here for Windermere—Lake Side, Newby Bridge and Conishead Priory.)

IS a place of considerable importance; it is pleasantly situated, and contains about 10,000 inhabitants. It is unquestionably an ancient town, but its aspect is modern, and it has been in many respects much improved in recent years. The Market Place occupies a central position at the junction of four principal streets, these are Market Street, King Street, Queen Street, and Daltongate; these and some other streets, no less important, contain plenty of attractive shops. It contains also a commodius Market House, and excellent hotels. The Parish Church is a

GENERAL VIEW OF ULVERSTON.

spacious building, consisting of nave, north and south aisles, and western tower, and though it is supposed to have been erected in the reign of Henry I., it has undergone so many reconstructions in the course of its history that the only ancient feature which it possesses is a fine Norman arch-way under a modern porch on the south side. It contains a large number of mural monuments, and stained glass windows, chiefly memorials of Furness families. The church is dedicated to St. Mary. Holy Trinity church is a modern structure, near the Railway Station. It was consecrated in 1832, but has materially altered since that date. There are also places of worship for various non-conformist bodies in different parts of the town. After the dissolution of Furness Abbey, Ulverston came to be regarded as the capital of Furness, its situation being peculiarly well adapted to meet the requirements of the surrounding district. Its commercial importance was perhaps greatest after the opening of the canal in 1795, but the development of Barrow has compelled it to acknowledge that great town as in many respects its superior. Situated as it is on the border of a rich iron ore district many of its inhabitants find employment in the mines; but it has also a few manufactures of its own. There are also several private residences in the neighbourhood; and its surroundings are extremely picturesque.

There are several places of interest in the vicinity of Ulverston, which a tourist should not fail to visit if time permit. One is Swarthmoor Hall, owing to its connection with George Fox, the founder of the Society of Friends. He was hospitably received by the then residents, Judge Fell and his wife Margaret, and permitted to hold meetings for worship in the hall. Margaret Fell joined the Society and underwent much persecution on that account. Some years after her

CHURCH WALK, ULVERSTON.

husband's death she contracted a second marriage, becoming the wife of George Fox. The Meetinghouse which Fox himself founded, is about half a mile distant from the Hall. It contains Fox's Bible, printed in 1541, his chair, and some other relics. Swarthmoor Hall is now occupied as a farmhouse. Other places worth visiting near Ulverston are Bardsea, a sea-side village, with an interesting church, an ancient tumulus, and other objects of antiquarian interest. Then there is Birkrigg Common, about three miles from Ulverston, from which a magnificent view is to be obtained, and on which various prehistoric remains exist. Urswick, which lies at the foot of Birkrigg, has also an ancient church which deserves a visit.

From Ulverston a branch line of railway runs to the foot of Windermere Lake, where a steamboat will be in readiness to convey the visitor to Bowness and Ambleside. A description of this route, and of the Circular Tours arranged by the Railway Company from Ulverston to some of the most attractive parts of the Lake District will be found on last page of cover.

ULVERSTON PARISH CHURCH.

PRINCES' STREET, ULVERSTON.

Ulverston people are somewhat inordinately proud of the fact that their town once produced a great man. Many "worthies" whose fame has not spread beyond the purlieus of

MEETING HOUSE, ULVERSTON.

the town, have flitted across the local stage, but Sir John Barrow's name is, or was, world-wide. Born on June 19th, 1764, in the little village of Dragley Beck, which is now practically

CANAL FOOT, ULVERSTON.

joined to Ulverston, in a humble straw-thatched cottage (still standing) he early displayed a decided inclination for mathematics. After spending some years at an iron foundry at Liver-

MARKET PLACE.

pool, he became mathematical master at a school at Greenwich, whence he was appointed secretary to the Embassy to China under Lord Macartney in 1792. Lord Macartney on his appointment to the government of the Cape of Good Hope, chose Mr. Barrow, as he then was, as his private secretary. He was subsequently appointed auditor-general of public accounts (or "accompts" as Mr. Barrow would have spelled the word). In 1804 Lord Melville appointed him secretary to the Admiralty from which post he retired in 1845. In 1835 he was created a baronet. He is the author of various treatises. He died November 28th, 1848. Sir John Barrow received his early education in the Old Town Bank Grammar School of Ulverston, which building is now, alas! used as a barn, a brand new edifice of monster proportions yclept the "Victoria Higher Grade School," having usurped its due functions. Grateful Ulverston honoured Sir John Barrow and itself by erecting to his memory a light-house-like column on Hoad Hill, an eminence that dominates the town.

HOAD MONUMENT.

Ulverston is not progressive, but a suburb to the town has sprung up which is styled South Ulverston. The inhabitants are for the most part, in the parlance of the towns-people, "off-comes." They are regarded with a somewhat pitying condescension by their conservative neighbours who have small sympathy with any initiative talents. In South Ulverston there are four distinct productive concerns. First and most important the North Lonsdale Iron and Steel Works, and in addition to these, a paper factory, chemical works, and a tannery. At Canal foot in South Ulverston is the old "crossing," where in days prior to the construction of the railway, the over-sands coaches used to arrive on *terra firma* from Lancaster. The office of the "Guide" is still in existence, but his duties, which are paid for by the Duchy of Lancaster and the Railway Company, now chiefly consist in directing Flookburgh fishermen's carts across the ever-shifting channel. Not far from canal foot is an

LEVY BECK.

old-fashioned round-chimneyed house, called Plumpton Hall, formerly a mansion of importance and repute, now a farmhouse. In days of yore it was the home of one of the branches of

SWARTHMOOR HALL, ULVERSTON.

the Sawrey family. It still contains a curious lantern said to be "dobby-haunted." Little rest and little happiness belongs to the fool-hardy person who takes any undue liberties with the said lantern. Nor will it leave its chosen abode. Take it where you will, aided by no mortal agency it regains the house.

Ulverston possesses branch offices of four important Banks—The Liverpool, The Lancaster, The Cumberland Union, and The London City and Midland. In the Ellers there is an old cotton mill which has been converted into a boot and shoe factory, and in Lightburne Road is an extensive printing establishment—The Otto Printing Works. As is natural in a town situated in the centre of an important agricultural area there are several prosperous corn mills in existence.

Within a short distance of Ulverston is Conishead Priory, once the home of the Doddings, from whom it passed by marriage to the Bradylls, Miss Sarah Dodding bestowing her hand,

WOODLAND DELL, ULVERSTON.

her heart, and her fortune upon John Bradyll, all of them without her mother's consent. It is now a Hydropathic Establishment, and is found to be a convenient centre for those who wish to spend some weeks in the Lake district, and at the same time to avoid the localities haunted by the general ruck of sight-seers. A 'bus conveys the visitors every Sunday to the Parish Church where they sit surrounded by the memorials of dead and gone Doddings and Bradylls.

On the rising ground to the North of the town an imposing mansion of modern structure is the residence of Myles Kennedy, Esq., the head of a family that owns important iron-ore mines in the vicinity. It bears the name of Stone Cross.

VIEW ON ULVERSTON SANDS.

LEVEN VIADUCT.

MESSRS. RANDALL & PORTER, LTD.,
Tanners and Leather Merchants,
Low Mill Tannery, ULVERSTON.

THE soundest and most reliable of leather only is manufactured by this firm, who enjoy a high reputation for the superior excellence of their make among some of the

largest buyers of this indispensable material in the home markets. Established in 1888 by Messrs. C. Randall and J. T. Porter, the business was converted into a private limited company in November, 1897, the board of directors comprising the following gentlemen: Chairman: Mr. Samuel Cooke, Scott Park, Burnley; Mr. R. O'Neil Pearson, Ulverston; Mr. George Randall, Bootle Tannery Company; Mr. J. T. Porter, who also acts as Secretary; Mr. C. Randall, Managing Director. The premises known as Low Mill Tannery, occupy an area of about 3½ acres in the west portion of the town, and comprise extensive yards and ranges of substantial buildings devoted to the various manufacturing departments, in the first-named are twenty spacious lime pits, and one hundred and fifty tan pits, in which the hides are placed and frequently turned in the liquor while undergoing this process. There are also large drying rooms, warehouses for finished stock, and other buildings in which are installed the requisite machines for striking, scouring, pinning and rolling leathers in the most improved modern methods, motive power being supplied by steam power. The best hides only are used, selected with care from the English, South American and Continental markets—principally Florence and Lisbon, and in their preparation the firm's leathers are strictly guaranteed free from all chemical processes and are warranted genuine tanned hides. These include the best sole leathers, butts, bends, offall, etc., and are supplied in steadily increasing quantities to the leading boot, shoe, and belt manufacturers in the chief seats of those industries in the kingdom, the firm having established an exten-

sive branch at Leicester, where they have a representative and warehouse for the wholesale business. Between fifty and sixty hands are employed in the tannery, under the competent supervision of Mr. Randall, the managing director, who, it is unnecessary to add, possesses a thoroughly practical and technical knowledge of every detail of the trade he so ably represents.

MESSRS. JOHN STONES LIMITED.

PATENT SHUTTER AND LIFT WORKS,

ULVERSTON.

THE old-established and well-known firm of John Stones Limited, reconstructed within recent years, now incorporates the businesses which were carried on by John Stones; Salmon, Barnes & Co.; A. Attwood & Co.; and the Ulverston Shutter & Lift Co. Ltd. Their freehold works, newly rebuilt, are situated about seven minutes distant from the Railway Station, at the west end of the town, and have been specially laid out for the trade and fitted with modern machinery with

every movement up-to-date.   One of the principal industries carried on is the construction of a New Folding Partition (Phillips' Patent) of which John Stones Limited are the exclusive makers. These are admirably adapted and extensively used in Schools, Class-rooms, Public Halls, etc. and have been adopted by the Admiralty in preference to others, and fixed at the Royal Naval College, Greenwich, and at Woolwich and other places.   In Ulverston these Patent Partitions may be seen at the Board Schools, Dale Street; the new Infant School, Church Walk; and the Working Men' Club, Church Walk.   The Company is now doing a large business in Patent Safety and Self-sustaining Lifts and Hoists for Hotels, Private Houses, Banks, Warehouses, etc., and the ease with which these can be manipulated and their freedom from any liability to get out of order, are rapidly raising them in the public estimation as evidenced in the steadily increasing trade. Their Revolving Shutters, too, of which they make a great variety in wood, iron and steel, are in great demand, and the contract for the requirements of the War Office is now in their hands. They have always sought a reputation for first-class work only, and it is evident they have spared, and are sparing, no effort to win it.   In all their specialities the best of materials only are employed, and reliable workmen fully conversant with their business are sent out to fix.   Medals have been awarded them at Exhibitions in London, Paris, Melbourne, Manchester, Bradford, York, Exeter, and Cork.   Since the retirement of Mr. John Stones in 1888, the Works have been under the management of their energetic secretary, Mr. E. Phillips.

MR. FREDERICK WILKINSON,

Colliery Agent and Coal and Coke Merchant,

County Chambers, ULVERSTON,

And New Road, SETTLE,

A VERY considerable proportion of the coal supplies distributed in Ulverston and throughout the Furness railway district is obtained through the agency of Mr. Frederick Wilkinson, whose business is one of the oldest of the kind in this part of the country. It was originally established

at Settle about fifty years ago by the predecessors of the present proprietor, who took over the concern in 1887 and has since largely increased the scope of the business transacted in both the wholesale and retail departments. Mr. Wilkinson's offices are centrally situated in County Chambers, Ulverston and New Road, Settle, Yorks., and there is provided every convenience for the head-quarters work connected with the various agencies at all the stations on the Midland, London and North Western, and Furness Railway, north of Skipton. At the Ulverston and Settle Stations where the Retail trade is carried on, are stored large stocks of household and steam coals of all classes which are supplied at the lowest current market prices. Mr. Wilkinson is agent for the Manvers Main Collieries Ltd., the accompanying illustration showing a view of the pit-head at the colliery at Wath-upon-Dearne, from which the enormous quantity of 30,000 tons is drawn weekly. A wide-spread and old-established wholesale and retail connection extends substantial and steadily increasing support to the proprietor, who is, it may also be mentioned, agent here for the Royal Fire and Life Insurance Company, one of the wealthiest offices in the country, having the large capital of £9,550,477.

Messrs. T. F. TYSON & SONS,

Builders, Contractors, Joiners, Wheelwrights, House Carpenters & Undertakers,

LIME KILN AND QUARRY OWNERS,

CHURCH WALK, ULVERSTON.

MANY of the largest and most important public and private building works executed within recent years in Ulverston and the Furness district have been carried out by Messrs. T. F. Tyson & Sons, the oldest firm of builders and contractors in this part of the country, whose extensive business also includes the various departments enumerated at the head of this notice. The firm's premises, situated in Church Walk, are close to the Parish Church, and occupy a considerable area of ground on both sides of the street. A well-appointed suite of offices adjoins the entrance to the principal yard, in which are erected spacious workshops for joiners, wheelwrights, blacksmiths, etc., with stores for materials of all descriptions, and a range of stabling and sheds for the numerous horses and vehicles required in the delivery of goods and for general haulage purposes. On the south side of the thoroughfare is another large yard, providing space for the stone working shed, in which is installed a powerful plant of the latest design, for cutting slabs or blocks of stone up to 9 ft. by 4 ft. by 4 ft., together with a complete equipment of wood-working machinery, comprising sawing, planing, mortising and other appliances driven by steam power for the manufacture of joinery and builder's fitments of every description. The accompanying views of the yards will convey an idea of the extent and completeness of the works

in the various departments, which give regular employment to between eighty and one hundred hands, including of course those engaged on outside contracts. The lime quarries and kilns situated at Plumpton, are similarly well-equipped for the work of production, and enable the firm

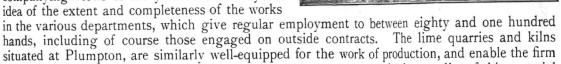

to obtain supplies of this material at first cost, a considerable advantage in estimating for large orders. Messrs. Tyson & Sons number amongst their extensive connection, the Earl of Derby, the Furness Railway Company, of which the Duke of Devonshire is Chairman, the Ulverston Urban District Council, and most of the principal local bodies. They are also contractors to Her Majesty's Government, and have also erected the Cottage Hospital, the Sun Hotel, Cattle Market, and gentlemen's mansions in the district, while in course of erection is the handsome building for the new Liverpool Bank. We may mention that Mr. A. Tyson, the eldest son of the head of the firm, and Mr. Wm. Fox, son-in-law, are the managing partners.

JOSEPH TAYLOR,

BRUSH MANUFACTURER,

Telegrams:—
Taylor, Brushmaker, Ulverston.

KING STREET, ULVERSTON.

WE give herewith a view of some of the different proceeds of brush manufacturing as seen on the establishment of Mr. Joseph Taylor, brush manufacturer, Ulverston, the business having been established by his grandfather in 1842; the establishment comprising two large warehouses and several workshops. Mr. Taylor is an expert in all matters connected with the trade, and enjoys a high reputation for supplying the best classes of articles at the lowest prices. A staff of fifteen or more hands is employed, under supervision of the principal, and a large annual output in the way of household, ship, mill, stable, brewers and other brooms and brushes, fancy and other baskets, etc., characterises the business. The list of articles manufactured is too long for enumeration here, but we may mention that price lists with full particulars are furnished on request. Mr. Taylor is the only brush manufacturer in the town. Ironmongers, grocers, &c., find it expedient to deal with him direct for all supplies in his line, satisfaction and good wearing qualities being guaranteed. Householders &c., when buying brushes from their respective houses can only rely on them being Taylor's make by seeing they are stamped with the trade mark.

C. PENNINGTON & SONS,

AGRICULTURAL ENGINEERS, MACHINISTS, &c.,

Queen Street, ULVERSTON.

WITH the recent additions in premises and with the improved plant laid down, Messrs. C. Pennington & Sons possess exceptional facilities for the execution of orders in every branch of agricultural engineering and machine work on the most efficient modern lines, of which they make a speciality of repairs to lawn mowers, and mangle rollers. Having been established for thirty years, the firm have all the advantages of a long practical experience, and as representatives of the leading makers of agricultural implements their stock will be found replete with all the latest improvements in this class of machinery, steam and gas engines, and plant of every description for milling and food-preparing processes. The large fitting shop is fully equipped with powerful machinery for manufacturing and repairing purposes, the firm having erected a patent lawn mower cylinder grinder, the only one of the kind in the district, motive force for which is supplied by a new gas engine laid down early in the year. Other new plant has also been installed in the recently-erected portion of the premises, while extensive space is now appropriated to the large and varied stock of new and second-hand machinery, chain, lift, and force pumps, washing, wringing and mangling machines, barrel, Princess, and tub churns and butter workers, separators, and constructional ironwork of every description. Several competent workmen are employed in the various branches, special attention being given to all kinds of repairs, which in every case are carried out under the close personal supervision of the partners, who guarantee the result as equal to new machinery in efficient and satisfactory working.

Messrs. HUDSON & CO.,

Wholesale and Retail Wine and Spirit Merchants,
Importers & Bonders of Foreign & British Spirits,

22, King Street and Buxton Place,
ULVERSTON.

FOR nearly a century the business of Messrs. Hudson and Co. has occupied a leading position in the Lake District, where the successive proprietors have established an old and influential family connection as Wholesale and Retail Wine and Spirit Merchants and Ale and Stout Bottlers and Agents. The premises, situated in one of the main thoroughfares of the town, comprise a spacious warehouse and stores, the latter, as will be seen from our illustration, being a well-appointed room conveniently arranged for this department of the business. In the cellars beneath, the firm have always on hand a large and well-selected stock of choice vintage ports, sherries, clarets, champagnes, and still and sparkling wines of the leading shippers, fine old Cognac brandies, the best blends of Irish and Highland whiskies and liquers, and Kimmond's ærated waters, for which they are agents. As agents for Bass and Co.'s world-famed Burton mild, pale and strong ales, Findlater's nourishing stout, and Rose's oatmeal stout, the firm are in a position to supply these leading brews either to the trade or for family consumers.

Mr. John Smith,

WHOLESALE AND RETAIL WINE AND SPIRIT MERCHANT,

Smith's Court, Lower Brook Street, ULVERSTON.

NOTWITHSTANDING the common belief that business concerns of prodigious age are frequently met with in this country, it is as a matter of fact comparatively rare to find one whose period attains

to a century in length; but this is the case with the business to which the present sketch is devoted. Established over a hundred years ago, a continuous and prosperous trade has been carried on in all kinds of the best wines and spirits. The premises are of a comfortable old-fashioned description, just off the main thoroughfare, and admirably suited for the trade. The different apartments, bar, office, sales-room, etc., are well furnished, and there is excellent warehouse accommodation. The stocks

held embrace all kinds of ports, sherries, clarets, champagnes, Maderias, Burgundies, and the like, the most famous vintages being represented; and also every sort of whisky, brandy, rum, gin, pure spirits, and so forth. The lines of malt beverages are especially full, including all the best-known names, such as Allsopp; beer, stout, and ale, being drawn from the wood. A large and well-established connection of good class is enjoyed in the district, the proprietor

having a high reputation for business-like dealing and knowledge of the trade.

Messrs. ROBINSON BROTHERS,

Bottlers, Wine & Spirit Merchants, Aerated Water Manufacturers and Importers,

Gill & Brook St., Ulverston.

ORIGINALLY founded in 1834 by the late Mr. Robert Robinson, this old-established concern was taken over in 1896 by the present proprietors, who then assumed the title of Robinson Brothers, and at the same time relinquished the brewing department, turning their attention exclusively to

those branches of the bottling trade which we have indicated at the head of this notice.   Known for generations as "Robinson's Gill Brewery," the premises have recently been re-constructed to include a splendidly equipped ærated water manufactory, for which plant has been laid down by the well-known firm of Dan Rylands, Ltd., Barnsley, which comprises all the latest improvements in machinery for the output of beverages of the highest quality and purity on the most modern and approved sanitary methods.   On this portion of the works is also the brewery for "STONE GINGER BEER," a much appreciated specialty of the firm's manufacture, the water for this and the ærated beverages being obtained from an excellent spring on the premises.   They are also in this department sole agents for "KENTORA," the original Hop Bitter Ale, and WHEATLEY'S HOP BITTERS.   As bottlers the firm are agents for Bass & Co's. PALE AND MILD ALES, sole agents for D'Arcy & Son's celebrated Dublin "Invalid" STOUT, and Barclay, Perkin's & Co's. London STOUT, all of which are also supplied in cask, as are also LIGHT TABLE AND STRONG ALES of the highest local repute.   On the WINE AND SPIRIT department Messrs. Robinson Brothers hold important agencies for Ulverston and district for Charles Mackinlay & Co's celebrated finest old cased Scotch Whisky, "V.O.B." special blend, and the famous "Bann" Whisky, a delicious Irish brand only supplied in bottles, the finest blends of old Scotch Whiskies, "Old Judge," the original "Mountain Dew," the "Oban" blend and fine old cased Irish Whisky.

BIRKETT'S

MILLINERY, DRESSMAKING, HOSIERY, GLOVE, MANTLE, JACKET & DRESS STORES,

COUNTY SQUARE, ULVERSTON.

MORE than 21 years ago Mr. T. Birkett commenced what in those days was quite a novelty in the town, viz. :—business conducted on the Cash system, that this principle has been appreciated by the general public is evidenced by the fact that he has gone on enlarging his premises, and increasing his trade, until now he occupies a foremost position in the Dry Goods trade of this district. Keeping a large staff of Tailors, Dressmakers and Milliners on the premises, he is fully prepared for any emergency. Mourning orders having special attention. The stock of Dress Materials shewn at this establishment comprises all the latest novelties of the seasons, also Prints, Galateas, Muslins, Blouse Materials, Etc. The Baby Linen, Ladies' and Children's Underclothing department which is in the spacious Show Room up-stairs, is fully stocked with a variety of goods in all the best makes. The Corset trade is evidently a big thing with them, having over 1000 pairs in stock. They do a very large letter order trade, and would be pleased to forward patterns on application.

Blankets, Flannels, Flannelettes, Sheets, Counterpanes, Table Linens, Tickings, Floor and Stair Oil Cloths, Lace Curtains, Art Muslins, Etc., are A1 value. The Tailoring and Ready-made Clothing Trade carried on at their New Market Street shop, has proved beyond doubt that the people of this district like a good article. We never saw a better class of Ready-made Clothing, and the prices so moderate. That Birkett's do a good Bespoke Tailoring trade is evident by the workmen employed in their Tailors workshops, (by the way the finest workrooms in the district).

Messrs. DICKINSON & SONS,

GROCERS, MILLERS, PROVISION DEALERS, ETC.,

Queen St., Neville Mill & Ure Mill, ULVERSTON, & Witherslack Mill, GRANGE.

Telephone No. 27, Ulverston.

ONE of the largest concerns of its kind in Ulverston and district is that to which we devote the following sketch, the business having been founded in 1858 and carried on, on progressive lines from the start. The chief business premises, in Queen Street, are commodious and well suited for the wide range of transactions undertaken by the firm, comprising offices, sale rooms, warehouses, etc., while they possess the best milling facilities in the three mills mentioned. The lines

of family groceries and supplies are specially comprehensive, and include all the usual articles in the way of tea and coffee, cocoa, flour, sugar, tinned and preserved meats, fish, fruits, and vegetables, sauces, spices, relishes, and condiments generally. Provisions are well represented in the best classes of hams, bacon, butter, cheese, eggs, lard, and the like. Soap of all kinds is also an important line, and also excellent and cool cellarage for butter and cheese. Flour, meal, grain, and provender are, as intimated, leading items in the business, and are supplied in the best qualities and at the lowest current prices. A special department is devoted to wines, spirits, and malt beverages, all the leading names and brands being represented. In the line of feeding specialities, the agency is held for the well-known "Bibby" cake and meal, the fine qualities of which for quick feeding and rich milk are highly appreciated by farmers and stock raisers generally. The Messrs. Dickinson have always made it a point to keep abreast of the times in all respects, and in their mills and business premises the fullest use is made of labour-saving appliances and improved machinery, they were the first concern in Ulverston to adopt the telephone (1880) and also the electric light (1885). A large staff is employed, and the most thorough organisation prevails in all departments, five or more horses being employed for outside work.

IN all lines, equitable prices are the rule. Orders receive prompt attention and are filled with the utmost care.

MR. HARGREAVES,

PHOTOGRAPHER.

Lightburne Road, ULVERSTON and DALTON=IN=FURNESS.

MANY of the illustrations of local objects of interest with which this section of our
"Holiday Resort Guide" is so freely embellished, are reproduced from views taken by Mr.
Hargreaves, whose skilful work as an art photographer will certainly commend them as a
most acceptable and attractive feature of the volume. Established since 1874 in the district.
Mr. Hargreaves has his principal studio in Lightburne Road, Ulverston, situated at the
west end of the town, and within a short distance of the railway station and post office,

facing the cattle market and drill hall, and on the way to Conishead Priory. The establishment occupies a corner site in this central position and comprises a spacious and well-furnished
reception room in which may be inspected a large selection of choice examples of high-class
portraits, groups and views in every form of modern photography, from the tiniest miniature,
to the handsome enlargements in carbon, platino-type and opal for which Mr. Hargreaves is
so widely noted as an expert specialist. The studio proper is a large and finely-lighted
apartment provided with a complete equipment of apparatus and accessories containing all the
most up-to-date improvements conductive to successful operative work in all branches of the
art. The difficult and delicate task of posing the sitters is undertaken personally by the
proprietor, or by a thoroughly reliable and skilful assistant, with the satisfactory result of
securing a life-like and perfect reproduction of features and physique so essential to photographic portraiture. Mr. Hargreave's studio at Dalton-in-Furness is equally well-equipped for
the purpose, and at both establishments an extensive and influential *clientile* evidence by their
substantial support the estimation in which this gentleman's professional services is held.

Mr. HENRY RILEY,

Draper, Silk Mercer, Milliner, Dressmaker, etc.,

26, New Market Street, ULVERSTON.

All the latest novelties for ladies' wear in every item of a fashionable in-door or out-door toilette are promptly introduced to local shoppers at Mr. Riley's well-known establishment, where he has always on hand a choice selection of new goods in mantles, costumes, jackets, furs and millinery suitably adapted for the requirements of the current season. Well situated in the new part of the town near the County Hotel and opposite the Market, Mr. Riley's premises have an attractive double-frontage, with large plate glass windows effectively dressed with a tasteful and varied assortment of goods indicating the leading lines held in the principal department. The establishment is well-appointed and is replete with a diversified general stock of drapery, silks, velvets, dress-pieces, laces, haberdashery and ladies' outfittings, corsets, lingerie, etc., which are displayed in the newest London and Continental styles. A staff of clever work-people is also employed on the premises in the execution of orders for dress and mantle-making, millinery and mourning outfits, the latter receiving close attention on the part of the proprietor, who exercises personal super-vision over each department of the business.

Telegrams: Court, Ulverston.

Mr. C. E. COURT,

WATCHMAKER, JEWELLER AND SILVERSMITH,

5, Market Place, ULVERSTON.

Situated in the very centre of the town in the best business thoroughfare, Mr. Court's handsome establishment is one of the most attractive features of the Market Place, where the business has been successfully carried on for the past forty years by the present proprietor and his predecessor, Mr. E. Hird. The premises have a pretty window-frontage, very effectively arranged with a varied and extensive assortment of elegant novelties in high-class gold and gem jewellery, ladies' and gentlemen's gold and silver watches, silver and electro plated ware, presentation plate and other articles decorative and useful, suitably adapted for wedding and birthday gifts, athletic club sports prizes or similar purposes. The stock also includes some interesting specialities of Mr. Court's own design in new patterns for souvenir spoons, one bearing the seal of Ulverston and the other a north view of Conishead Priory. These novelties, needless to say, have found popular favour with visitors in the district, who can thus secure at a trifling cost a most artistic reminder of their pleasurable sojourn in the neighbourhood. An excellent selection of optical goods is also on hand.

MR. JAMES ATKINSON,

PRINTER, PUBLISHER, STATIONER, BOOKBINDER, Etc.,

The Caxton Printing Works, ULVERSTON; and GRANGE-OVER-SANDS.

ESTABLISHED 1838.

THE principal establishment of its kind in Ulverston and district is unquestionably that of Mr. James Atkinson, to which we have pleasure in devoting the following notice.

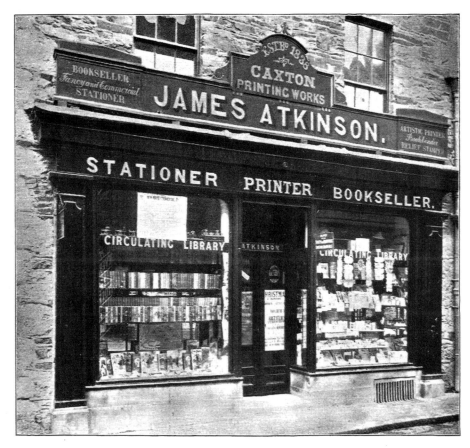

As will be noted, the frontage is double, the windows making an exceptionally attractive display of stock. The interior of the shop and sales department is well fitted and commodious, and a large and varied assortment of wares is maintained in all branches of the business. Bookselling forms an important feature, and an extensive stock is held of the best standard works in fiction, history, travels, and general literature. There is also a good Circulating Library, which is largely patronised by the community. All the usual lines of Plain and Fancy Stationery for commercial and general purposes, with Account Books, Journals, etc., and all the usual accessories of the trade, are kept in large quantities, together with an exceptionally attractive stock of Fancy Goods for presents and the like, this department, in fact, is a leading feature of the business, and persons wishing to secure really acceptable presents for Christmas, the New Year, Birthdays, etc., should not fail to call at the establishment and inspect the selection—it includes everything in the way of Fancy Articles, Leather Goods, Birthday Cards, Colour Books, Photo Frames, and similar articles.

The Printing Department is necessarily important. The proprietor has the best facilities in the way of modern machinery, new and artistic type, etc., for executing the highest class of printing at very low prices. He makes a specialty of printing from "Process" Engraved blocks, Invoice Headings, Memo. and Account headings, Wedding, Visiting, and "at Home" Cards, Ball Programmes, and in fact every description of printing, and publishing, his connection extending as far as London and Edinburgh. A staff of twenty-five or more is employed, and extensive premises in Brook Street, connected by telephone, are utilized as a Paper Warehouse, manufacturing Paper Bags, and for the wholesale trade.

Mr. JOHN BOULTON,

SADDLER and HARNESS MANUFACTURER,

Licensed Dealer in Game, etc.,

3, MARKET PLACE, ULVERSTON.

WE give a view herewith of this well-known establishment, which is without question the most extensive of its class in the district. The business dates from the year 1851, and is carried on in commodious premises in one of the leading thoroughfares of the town, a very handsome display being made in the various lines handled. The stock of saddles, harness, bits, bridles, whips, spurs, etc., with the usual sundries of the trade, is distinctly up-to-date and attractive, the articles being well designed and made in the best manner from the most serviceable materials. Everything required by persons keeping horses for farming purposes, business, or pleasure, is kept on hand, and in qualities to suit customers. Other lines comprise portmanteaus, travelling trunks, hat boxes, Gladstone and kit bags, machine belts, etc. As noted, Mr. Boulton is a licensed dealer in game, all kinds being supplied in season; he also keeps a large and excellent stock of guns, rifles, revolvers,

and the like, with every sort of cartridges for breech loading guns, and all kinds of sporting ammunition. The connection is well established in all branches, the articles being of guaranteed quality and offered at moderate prices.

Mr. THOMAS IDDON,

Tailor and Draper,

11 & 26, Market Street, ULVERSTON.

THE premier position in Ulverston in the lines indicated above is undoubtedly held by Mr. T. Iddon, of the numbers mentioned in Market Street. The principal drapery establishment is at No. 11, immediately opposite the Sun Hotel, the shop having a handsome double front and making an attractive show in the windows. In all, four storeys are utilised for the business, large and well-selected stocks being held in the different departments.

From time to time, exceptional opportunities are offered to purchasers for obtaining supplies in the various lines handled. Mantles, capes, jackets, costumes, skirts, waterproofs, etc., together with blouses and summer shirts, sunshades and umbrellas, all the newest materials for dresses, with prints, fancy cotton goods, household and furnishing drapery, fancy goods and trimmings, and like articles, may be had at really extraordinary prices. Especial bargains are repeatedly offered in superior classes of cashmeres, serges, poplins, foules, and silk and wool fabrics of all kinds, and also in galateas, zephyrs, fancy muslins, silk grenadines, sateens, and the like. Tapestry and Brussels, Kidder, Axminster, and other carpets.

DENTAL SURGERIES,

A communications to be
addressed to
Mr. THOMAS HARRISON.

22, Cavendish Street, ULVERSTON.

CONTEMPORARY with the general advance made in all branches of surgical science during the nineteenth century, the practice of dentistry has been greatly improved within recent years both in its operative methods, and in the perfect system now adopted by the expert specialist to supply nature's deficiencies in cases of decay arising from various causes peculiar perhaps to the age in which we live. Among the leading practitioners in the Ulverston district few enjoy a higher reputation for skilful treatment than the operator in charge of the above Dental Surgeries, Mr. C. W. Williams, Dentist Surgeon, whose extensive experience gleaned at the Dental and Charing Cross Hospitals, London, is sufficiently indicated in his connection with such well-known institutions as we have just named. The Dental Surgeries, situated at 22, Cavendish Street, Ulverston, close to the County Hotel, are under the personal superintendence of Mr. Williams, and are fully and efficiently equipped with every modern convenience for the practice of high-class dentistry. The most improved modern apparatus has been introduced by the proprietor for extractions under gas, which are made a speciality, and other leading features are the care and attention given to children's teeth, gold fillings, crown, bar and bridge work. This, it should be mentioned, is the only establishment where all the latest improvement in high-class dental work are undertaken nearer than Lancaster and Liverpool, thus supplying a much-appreciated convenience to residents in the neighbourhood. Artificial teeth of the best quality, made to suit all classes are manufactured on the premises and as this work is executed under the practical supervision of Mr. Williams a perfect fit is invariably guaranteed in all cases. Consultations and advice are placed at the disposal of clients free of charge, Mr. C. W. Williams being in daily attendance for this purpose.

Mr. G. G. WHITE,

Gentlemen's Hosier, Glover, Hatter and Outfitter,

18, New Market Street, ULVERSTON.

And at BARROW and GRANGE-OVER-SANDS.

ESTABLISHED over twenty-five years ago, the above business is one of the best known and most flourishing in the district. The Ulverston premises, to which this notice chiefly refers, are conveniently situated in a leading street, and, as our illustration shows, have an attractive double frontage with a good window space. The interior arrangements are commodious, and a large and well-assorted stock is always kept in the various lines indicated. The several departments include hats and caps by the best makers, shirts of all classes, juvenile goods of different kinds, hosiery wares, gloves, and general fancy articles. The lines of silk and felt hats are specially excellent and up-to-date, both as to style and price, caps in all the newest patterns and materials being a specialty. Dress shirts, French print, Indian

gauze, flannel and tennis shirts, are supplied in all qualities; all the latest novelties in boys' ready-made clothing are kept and sent on approval to any address; lambs' wool, natural llama, and merino in all weights in shirts and drawers, hose and half-hose in great variety as to quality and material are always on hand.

The Misses J. & E. HARRISON,

Confectioners, Pastrycooks, and Caterers,

20, KING STREET, ULVERSTON.

the tastefully appointed, and well-supported confectionery of the Misses J. & E. Harrison, which occupies an excellent position in one of the main thoroughfares of the town, where a very substantial and influential business has been carried on for the best part of the century just ended. The premises are of somewhat old-fashioned appearance having a double window frontage, and comprising in addition to the neatly-appointed shop, spacious refreshment rooms on the first floor, where teas, luncheons, etc., are served daily to visitors. A capital modern bakery is attached to the establishment, fitted with improved ovens, and here are turned out high-class bread, cakes, pastry, etc., under conditions leaving nothing to be desired on the score of sanitation and absolute cleanliness. The Misses Harrison are widely noted for their specialities in bridecakes of delicious quality, which are supplied to order from 10/- to £20, and other leading lines are made in jellies, creams, blancmanges, ices and other tempting delicacies included in the manufactures of a high-class confectioner's business.

FAMILIAR alike to residents and visitors in the district of which Ulverston is the centre, is

Mr. JOSEPH POSTLETHWAITE,

**Linen and Woollen Draper and Silk Mercer,
Mantle and Dressmaker,
Hatter, Hosier, and Gentlemen's Outfitter,**

King Street, ULVERSTON.

THIS well-known establishment dates from the year 1859, and is the oldest drapery business

conducted by the principal, and hence has been over forty years in existence. The premises are centrally situated in the main thoroughfare of Ulverston, and in every way suited for the requirements of the trade, two excellent double-fronted shops and two floors being utilised for the business. This, as set forth, includes all the usual lines of linen and woollen drapery, silk mercery, hats and caps, hosiery and gloves, and general outfitting; mantles, jackets, and dressmaking, forming a leading specialty. Two large and well-fitted show rooms are devoted to the mantles, dressmaking, etc., and a staff of twenty or more employed in this department, about thirty persons being employed by the business as a whole. Other lines comprise silks, velvets, dresses, waterproofs, furs, umbrellas, hosiery, gloves, corsets, ribbons, Swiss embroidery, laces, and the like. Improved lock-stitch sewing machines are also supplied on the best terms. Liberal arrangements are made for supplying clothing clubs, and every requisite for family mourning is kept on hand.

Messrs. CASSON & HARRISON,

**Auctioneers & Valuers,
Auditors, Arbitrators, & Accountants, Etc.,**

County Chambers, ULVERSTON.

THE important part played in all industrial and commercial communities by the auctioneer and valuer is too well known to need comment. In Ulverston and the surrounding district, the indispensable functions in question have long been performed by Messrs. Casson and Harrison, whose new and handsomely-appointed offices in the County Chambers occupy a central position opposite the County Hotel and near the Post Office and Market. The firm have had wide and valuable experience in all branches of the profession, and undertake every description of business as auctioneers and valuers, auditors, arbitrators. accountants, etc., and as property, estate, insurance, and general commission agents. Valuations for probate or transfer are carefully prepared, and rents of all kinds collected, periodical sales being held of every sort of household, farm, hotel, and other property, either at their rooms or at other places. As house agents, complete lists of furnished and unfurnished houses, country seats, mansions, etc., being kept for the assistance of patrons. Scrupulous care is given to all matters entrusted to the firm and satisfaction guaranteed. We may add that the business,

which dates from 1862, holds without question the premier position of its kind in the district.

F. E. KITCHIN,

COVENT GARDEN FRUIT STORES,

Brogden Street & Market Hall, ULVERSTON.

FRUIT and VEGETABLES, which are the necessaries of healthful life.—Covent Garden Fruit Stores are daily supplied with choice and fresh vegetables from the growers. Also fresh flowers, ferns, sprays, bouquets, wreaths, and flowers for table decorations. All the earliest fruits in season can be obtained at the above stores, and nothing could be more beneficial to

the general health than the natural juices of fresh fruit, their healthful and refreshing power is quickly recognised by invalids and the essence called the elixir of life. Most people who have seen the peach, nectarine, muscatel, and strawberry growing in large quantities, have been struck with the magnetic correspondence with all the powers of nature; they show the life of the earth and the sky, and have sunshine in their veins and dew in their cells.

FLOWERS.—It is because flowers are such lovely emblems of innocence, so like the merry faces of childhood, that they have a large place in our best affections. The beautiful varieties "The Covent Garden Fruit Stores" have to chose from will satisfy the wants of all.

> Oh, lovely flowers! the earth's rich diadem,
> Emblems are ye of heaven and heavenly joy,
> And starry brilliance in a world of gloom ;
> Peace, innocence, and guileless infancy
> Claim sisterhood with you, and holy is the tie.

Wedding and dinner parties supplied with all fruits and flowers possible to get.

Mr. W. H. RILEY,

Watchmaker and Jeweller,

38, Queen Street, ULVERSTON.

A VERY wide range of useful and ornamental articles in the way of watches, clocks, and jewellery, may be inspected at the above establishment, in Queen Street, Ulverston, of which Mr. W. H. Riley is the proprietor. The business dates from 1881, and is carried on on popular lines, the prices being suited to the means of all classes. The shop, of which we give a view, is in the leading thoroughfare of the town, and easily accessible. The stocks held are of a comprehensive description, including gold and silver watches, marble, gilt, bronze and wooden clocks, gold and gem jewellery, rings, pins, brooches, chains, bracelets, wedding rings, and in fact the whole range of jewellers' articles. The quality is excellent and the prices moderate in all lines. A noted speciality of the business is the repairs of all kinds of scientific instruments Mr. Riley having had great experience in this department. He gives the business his personal attention and executes all orders with the utmost care and despatch. We may mention that he is agent for the Temperance Hall Trust.

Mr. A. McCAIG,

(LATE MASON BROTHERS)

General Drapery, Millinery, Mantle, Dressmaking and Tailoring Establishment.

1 & 3, Market Place, & 1 & 3, Daltongate, ULVERSTON.

WE have pleasure in giving herewith a view of the principal establishment of Mr. A. McCaig, general draper, etc., of Ulverston. The premises are centrally situated in the leading business street of the town, near the Sun Hotel and the Market Hall, the frontage being attractive and well displayed. The different show rooms are spacious and well fitted, and a very choice display of goods is made in all departments. Millinery and dressmaking are the chief specialties, commodious show rooms upstairs being devoted to this branch. As a whole, the stock is admirably selected and suited for modern popular requirements, the various lines comprising, as set forth, general drapery, millinery, and mantle and dressmaking, an efficient staff being employed as assistants and in the work rooms. Excellent bargains are always obtainable in flannels and blankets, quilts, cotton and linen sheets, tickings, cottons, table linens and cloths, hollands, coatings, tweeds, dress goods, silks, trimmings, shirtings, skirtings, curtains,

gloves and umbrellas, the turnover being rapid and enabling fresh goods to be had in often.

Messrs. J. B. KAY & Co.,
Waterproof and Travelling Goods Depot, etc.,
9, King Street, ULVERSTON.

THE largest depot in Ulverston and district for the supply of the articles mentioned in our heading, is, without question, that of Messrs. J. B. Kay and Co., at No. 9, King Street, in the town named. The premises, as shown by our illustration, have a good double frontage and make a compendious display in the different lines held. These include everything in the way of the best kinds of sewing, knitting, and washing machines, and other domestic utensils; waterproof and oilskin clothing, leggings, carriage aprons, horse covers, fishing and other waterproof boots, stocking and trousers, nursery aprons and the like; together with air and water beds, cushions, elastic stockings, and all kinds of indiarubber and gutta percha surgical articles. Bassinettes and mail carts in all the latest designs. A large and splendid stock is also kept in the way of ladies' and gentlemen's umbrellas, which are offered at extremely moderate prices. Perhaps the chief speciality of the business is the supply of Waterproof clothing of different kinds, a large business being transacted in this department alone. The stock as a whole is of a very high class and of guaranteed excellence.

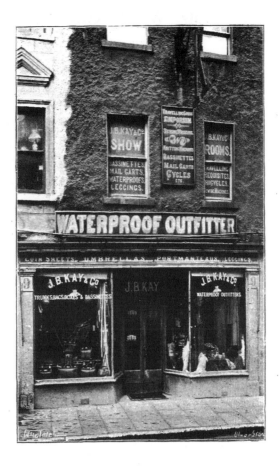

Mrs. WHITHAM,
Printer, Stationer, Bookseller & Newsagent,
47, Market Street, ULVERSTON.

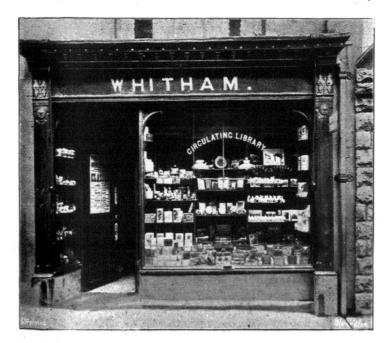

A very tasteful and attractive display of useful and artistic articles is invariably on view at the well-known establishment of Mrs. Whitham, which for upwards of twenty years has been a favourite depôt for all kinds of stationery, books, and the usual branches of newsagency and printing business. With these are also combined an excellent circulating library, well-stocked with some hundreds of volumes of entertaining literature, which may be obtained at a moderate charge by subscribers resident or visiting in the town. All the principal London and provincial journals, magazines, periodicals, etc., are received daily and distributed on the arrival of the early trains, and among the prominent features of the general stock are a widely varied assortment of local views and photographs of all celebrities of the day. The shop is centrally situated in the main thoroughfare of the town, and presents a prettily arranged window frontage in which are offered for inspection choice specimens of W. H. Goss's heraldic porcelain china, for which Mrs Whitham is sole agent in town.

THE ULVERSTON REMNANT WAREHOUSE COMPANY, LTD.,
Corner of Soutergate & Church Walk, ULVERSTON.

AMONGST the largest drapery establishments in Ulverston, the above concern merits special mention in a work of this kind. It represents an enterprise of considerable standing which was formed into a limited liability company in 1893, Mr. Thomas Briggs, Mr. W. Isherwood, Mr. H. Greenhalgh, and Mr. Thomas Hamnett, being the proprietors. The structure utilised for the business, of which we give a view herewith, occupies a prominent position and is in all respects well adapted for the trade carried on. This comprises all the usual lines of drapery (both plain and fancy), dresses and dress materials, mantles and jackets, cloaks, mackintoshes, ladies' under-clothing, hosiery, ready-made clothing, and a large number of articles more or less directly connected with the business. Remnants and odd pieces are of course a special feature, but bargains are offered in all lines. Nearly all goods supplied by the Company are bought direct from the mills for cash, and all are sold at the lowest possible price, the cash principle also being

adopted in selling the wares. It is not too much to say that the Company keep one of the largest stocks of ladies' and girls' jackets, capes, and costumes in the district ; while in addition to the general stock all kinds of infants' outfits, underclothing, perambulators and mail carts, are supplied. The ready-made clothing department is already an important feature and is daily gaining in the public favour. Very large lines are always held in remnants of calico, sheeting, linen, flannelettes, scarlet and white flannels, prints, linings, dress materials, velveteens, etc,. and a large stock is unquestionably held in bedsteads, spring and flock mattresses, and flock and feather bedding. Special lots are offered from time to time, slightly damaged table and bed linen being not infrequently disposed of in large quantities at marvelously low prices. Boys,' Men's, and Youths' clothing are made to measure at moderate figures.

The Remnant Warehouse Co., Limited, offers great advantages to all persons needing any of the supplies mentioned. The stocks are always varied and attractive and well repay the visitor's time.

Mr. FRANCIS TOWN,
General Draper, Silk Mercer and Ladies' Outfitter,
12, King Street, ULVERSTON.

ALTOGETHER of a high-class grade, the business now conducted by Mr. Francis Town is of old-established standing, although, it should be added, there is nothing of the old-fashioned to be ascribed to the up-to-date methods upon which the concern is now carried on. Ample justification for this statement will be found in a glance at the attractively arranged display in the window of the establishment, in which may be inspected all the latest novelties and smartest styles in vogue for ladies' wear, together with a large and well-selected assortment of fancy, general and furnishing drapery of which we may quote the following as the specialities: English and foreign dress fabrics in the newest designs and favourite shades; ladies' fashionable tailor-made coats and skirts, ladies' underclothing and corsets including the popular "C.B." make, an extensive range of skirts, "Shamrock" Irish ilnens and handkerchiefs, special novelties in made-up lace goods, Cash's cambric frillings, and "Sandown" suits for boys a higher grade speciality at moderate prices. The establishment occupies a central position, and provides every convenience for the transaction of a business.

Mr. THOMAS AFFLECK,
SCULPTOR, MONUMENTAL and GENERAL MASON,
Dragley Beck Lane, ULVERSTON.

THE above important branch of industry, of which Mr. Thomas Affleck is the local representative, dates from about fifty years back, and holds a well-established position in the town. The premises are conveniently situated in Dragley Beck Lane, and comprise the usual structures and appliances for the business, the latest machinery being employed for sawing limestone, etc. An excellent and thoroughly artistic display is made in the way of monumental sculpture, the designs being in admirable taste, and evincing a high degree of talent and accurate knowledge of the art on the part of the proprietor. This is evident in other branches of his work as well, including designs for pulpits, fonts, reredos, and the like. The business is well established, and of the highest class, the connection extending throughout the district. Designs and prices in all departments, in marble, granite, and limestone, are submitted on application, and satisfaction guaranteed.

Mr. RICHARD KENDALL, ✎✎✎

Furnishing Ironmonger,

✎✎✎ 27, KING STREET, ULVERSTON.

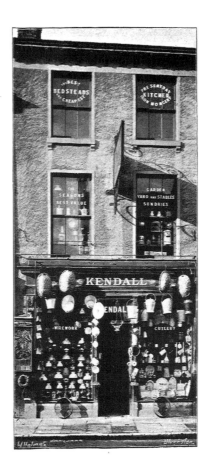

WE give herewith a view of Mr. Kendall's well-known ironmongery establishment, in King Street, Ulverston, which for nearly seventy years has held an important position among local business concerns. As shown, the premises have a good frontage and offer the best facilities for displaying stock, the exhibition of wares being always of a very comprehensive character. The upper floors are utilised for the business, and very large stocks are held in all departments. Our space forbids a complete or even partial enumeration of the goods handled, but it need not be said that all branches of ironmonger's supplies, and especially furnishing ironmongery, are well represented. The range of requisites in all departments is exceptionally wide, embracing all kinds of household utensils, culinary and other; carpenters' and joiners' tools; cutlery; washing, wringing, and other machines; pots, pans, dishes, tins, and the like; hall and hand lamps, and in fact everything associated with the trade. The premises form a veritable emporium of ironmongery and kindred supplies, and offer the best bargains to persons furnishing houses or in need of additional household articles. We should add that Mr. Kendall is also an extensive iron and steel merchant, and maintains large stores of the best classes of metal of the kind, this department perhaps being the speciality of the business. The connection is well established and extends throughout the district.

Mr. STAMPER, R.D.S,,

Surgeon=Dentist,

16 Queen St., ULVERSTON; & 18 St. George's

Terrace, MILLOM.

THE first to introduce into his practice in Ulverston, the use of anæsthetic agents for the painless extraction of teeth. Mr. Stamper, who possesses the full qualification of a registered dental surgeon with a London certificate, has adapted all the latest approved modern methods which long practical experience has demonstrated the most efficient for operative purposes. He undertakes every branch of dental practice with delicacy and expert skill, his speciality being the manufacture of artificial teeth, which are supplied at prices to suit all classes, and which may be commended as the perfection of easy fit, comfort and durability, sets of teeth can be fixed in the mouth in a few days after the mouth is prepared. All instruments used are thoroughly sterilized after each operation. Mr. Stamper is in attendance at his house in Queen Street, Ulverston, from 10 to 7 on Tuesdays, Wednesdays, Thursdays and Saturdays; and at 18, St. George's Terrace, Millom, on Mondays from 11-30, when patients can consult him free on all matters connected with dentistry in all the branches in which he is an expert.

Mr. Stamper claims to be the most successful tooth-extractor in the district.

Miss M. FRANCE,

FANCY DRAPER and SILK MERCER,

29, KING STREET, ULVERSTON.

THE latest and most fashionable novelties in every item of a lady's smart and up-to-date toilette are tastefully displayed in the prettily arranged shop-windows of Miss France's establishment, which has recently been opened by that lady with every prospect of securing a substantial share of public patronage in Ulverston and the district. The premises, centrally and conveniently situated at the above address have a neat double frontage and well-appointed interior well-stocked with every description of fancy drapery and silk mercery, together with an extensive assortment of stylish golf capes, dressing gowns, umbrellas, Dent's gloves, hosiery, ladies' underwear and articles of lingerie in all the latest styles, "C.B." corsets, and other details of feminine outfitting for out-door and in-door wear. A nicely furnished show-room in the rear of the shop is also devoted to the display of millinery, costumes, etc.

ABBEY SAUCE.

MAKES AN IMPRESSION

THE ABBEY SAUCE CO.,

King Street, ULVERSTON.

AMONG the more recent competitors for public favour, as a welcome addition to our table equipment, few articles in the form of condiments have met with more immediate and distinct success than Braithwaite's "Abbey Sauce," pronounced by connoisseurs and gourmets a delicious and appetising relish for game, fish, soups, hot and cold joints, chops, steaks, etc. This sauce was only placed on the market for the first time in 1897, and at once struck the popular taste, orders commencing to flow in from all parts of England, Scotland and Ireland, where it has become as familiar as household words, as the perfection of a nutritious relish, a stimulating and valuable tonic. The Abbey Sauce is put up in bottles with a tasteful and effective label, and is supplied in two sizes, at 6d. & 1/-, to be obtained from all grocers, &c., throughout the United Kingdom. The firm are also manufacturers of the "Abbey Baking Powder," a preparation which ensures pastry made with it very light and easily digested. The baking powder is sold in tins at 4d., 8d., and 1/4. Only the purest and best ingredients are used in preparing these specialities, which command a very extensive and rapidly growing sale.

Mr. FRED TODD,
Painter, Decorator, Sign Writer, Paperhanger, etc.,
The Gill, ULVERSTON.

WE have elsewhere had occasion to remark upon the spread of artistic taste and knowledge throughout the country generally, as particularly exemplified in the care bestowed on house decoration and kindred matters. The above establishment is evidence that the picturesque town of Ulverston is not behind others in this respect, the business having been founded by the father of the proprietor in the year 1872. The shop and sales room is centrally situated in the "Gill," and as our illustration shows, has a pleasing frontage and makes an attractive display in the usual lines of the trade. Very large and distinctively artistic stocks are maintained in the way of colours, wall-papers, interior decorations of all kinds (such as Lincrusta, Walton, Anaglypta, and the like), and also plain and ornamental glass, picture frames, oils, paints, etc., Mr. Todd being a gilder, glazier, and picture-frame

maker, as well. A large and well-established connection is enjoyed in the town and throughout the district, the proprietor having an excellent reputation for the high character of his work in all departments of the business. His prices and charges are moderate, and satisfaction is guaranteed in any work undertaken.

Mr. J. H. BENSON,
Corn Merchant, etc.,
5, King Street, ULVERSTON;
And Ellers Corn Mills.

ESTABLISHED in the year 1839, the above business is one of the oldest and best-known of its kind in the district. The shop and sales department is centrally situated in King Street, Ulverston, where very large stocks are held in all branches of the trade, the establishment having long enjoyed a high reputation for the finest sorts of flour, oatmeal, oatcake, "Friends' Oats," and the like staples. Large lines are also held in the way of feeding stuffs, feeding cakes, dog-biscuits, poultry foods and spices, bird seeds, agricultural seeds, and supplies all other necessaries in the interest of owners of stock. The agency is held for the noted "Albion Cakes," for which a great demand exists throughout the district. At the Ellers Corn Mills an experienced miller is employed, and particular success has always attended his efforts in making up farmers' grain for different purposes. None but articles of the best kind are stocked, and a high reputation is enjoyed for all classes of supplies with the farming community. The connection is well-established, and extends throughout the district, Mr. Benson being well known to a large circle of acquaintances and friends by whom he is much respected.

Mr. W. HOLMES,

Letterpress and Lithographic Printer, Stationer, &c.,

OTTO PRINTING WORKS,

ULVERSTON.

SOME exceptionally fine specimens of the Caxtonian art in its most up-to-date style have been issued from the above-named establishment, one of the most successful and flourishing industrial enterprises in this part of the country. The business dates back to its foundation in

CORNER OF MACHINE ROOM.

1876, when it was commenced on a comparatively modest scale by Mr. Holmes, who has since continuously developed the concern by opening up new departments among which are now included special features in chromo-lithography in all its branches, photo-engraving, art printing, book-binding and catalogue printing, the latter a very important speciality feature of the house. The premises known as the "Otto Printing Works" comprise a commodious building erected some five or six years ago, situated near the public Cattle Market and within five minutes distance of the station. The works are completely up-to-date with all the latest improvements in plant and appliances. The establishment is lighted throughout by an electric installation and heated with hot water pipes, and ventilated with one of Southwell's revolving fans, and as indicating the extent of business transacted it may be mentioned that a permanent staff of about seventy hands is employed in the various departments, among whom are several artists expert in designing catalogue covers and illuminating. In reference to this class of work we may quote the following testimony of leading journals in their criticism of "A Pilgrimage to the Saga

CORNER OF MACHINE ROOM.

Steads of Iceland," price 30/-, printed at these works, *The Manchester Guardian*:—"It would be unjust not to praise Mr. Holmes for his excellent rendering of the water colour drawings of Mr. Collingwood, Ulverston deserves credit for turning out such excellent work." *Liverpool Courier*:—"The result is a handsome book of fascinating interest, in which the capital sketches have been splendidly reproduced, the coloured plates in particular being veritable works of art." He is also the printer of the Reporter's Journal, The Shorthand Magazine, The Shorthand Writer and North Lonsdale Magazine. The latest work issued from this press is "The Art and Craft of Garden Making," by T. Mawson, price 21/-

The County Hotel,

Telephone No. 33.   ## ULVERSTON.

Proprietor = = Mr. THOS. BAINES.

Mr. T. Baines, who has just succeeded Mrs. Smith who for many years presided over the above Hotel, was for 12 years proprietor of the Scawfell Hotel, Rosthwaite, Keswick, and he is sure to keep up the popularity of this well known and comfortable house. The bright and attractive appearance outside, indicates the comfort and good appointment of the interior, which comprises spacious Bedroom Accomodation, Coffee Room, Reading Room, Ladies' Drawing Room, Commercial Room and handsome Billiard Room with two tables.   The Tariff is moderate and inclusive terms are made by the day or week.   The catering is well known in the past and under Mr. Baines will no doubt easy keep up to its high level.

POSTING.—Mr. Baines has a most complete and extensive establishment in this department, Waggonettes, Landaus, Victorias, Dogcarts, of smart appearance and well horsed can be obtained at the shortest notice, and visitors desiring to view this charming locality should consult Mr. Baines as to the excursion and view the handsome vehicles he can place at their disposal.

The Commercial arrangement for gentlemen are of the best, and the house has stood very high for many years amongst Commercial Hotels, the Commercial Room being especially large and well fitted and with a very pleasant view over the garden.

THE SUN HOTEL,

TELEPHONE
No. 052.

ULVERSTON.

MRS. WALKER, PROPRIETRESS.

The Sun Hotel is the oldest in Ulverston and although the oldest it is thoroughly up-to-date in the comfort of its appointments and conveniences.   It is conveniently situated for Commercial men in the very centre of the town.   To the many visitors who flock to Ulverston in the touring

season Mrs. Walker's Hotel is the favorite resting place, the Bedroom Accomodation is up-to-date and in addition to the well appointed Coffee Room there is a Ladies' Drawing Room.   There are also Reading, Smoking and Billiard Rooms, and excellent Commercial Room.   The Cuisine has always been a strong point at the Sun.   The wine list comprises many excellent brands. The Tariff generally is on a most moderate scale; when the excellence of the accomodation is taken into account.   There are good Stock Rooms for travellers.

Adjoining the Hotel are the Livery Stables where posting in all branches is catered for and vehicles of all kinds can be obtained.   Wedding and other orders are promptly attended to.

LAKE SIDE and NEWBY BRIDGE.

IN the pictures we are endeavouring to give in these pages, whether by the pen or by the photograph, it is by no means our intention to usurp the indispensable functions of the local guide; therefore we purposely avoid the attempt to be exhaustive.

From many charming nooks and corners in the immediate neighbourhood of these two places in question our readers must refer to the source indicated.

LAKE SIDE STATION, WINDERMERE.

The Furness Railway have a station at Lake Side it being the terminus of the branch line from Ulverston. It is from here that the steam yachts start on their tour to Ambleside, calling at the various piers on the Lake, from which every point of interest in the neighbourhood may be reached.

LAKE SIDE, LOOKING NORTH.

It should not be omitted to mention here that Mr. Robinson, of the New Lake Side Hotel, runs his char-a-bancs in connection with the Company's train service during the season.

NEWBY BRIDGE. The waters which flow under Newby Bridge have passed through some of the most romantic and delightful scenery in the kingdom.

Newby Bridge with the many attractions associated with it, is at the conjunction of the Lake with the river Leven, about seven-eighths of a mile from Lake Side Station and 9 miles by road from Ulverston.

The pictorial art which has made this village and district familiar to thousands who have never visited the spot are to be touched on in these pages.

NEWBY BRIDGE.

It is difficult to imagine a more delightful sanatorium and place of residence during the season than the Swan Hotel, the position is an ideal one, the establishment being a very old coaching house but thoroughly up-to-date.

SWAN HOTEL, NEWBY BRIDGE,

At the foot of Windermere Lake.

Within a mile of Lake Side Station and Steamboat Pier of the Furness Railway.

Seven miles from Grange-over-Sands, nine miles from Ulverston, and ten miles from Windermere (L. & N. W.).

Postal Address—Swan Hotel, Newby Bridge, Ulverston.   Telegrams · "REVELL, NEWBY BRIDGE."
Goods Address—Lake Side, F.R.

'Bus meets all Trains.   Improved Service of through Trains to (Windermere) Lakeside, F.R., via Carnforth.

Sanitation Perfect.   Spacious Coffee Room.   Table D'hote, separate Tables.   Luncheon and Afternoon Teas a Speciality.

POSTING.   BOATING.   FISHING (Salmon, Trout, Char, Pike, Perch).

PRIVATE GROUNDS extend for ¼-mile on the margin of the Lake.   LOVELY PANORAMIC VIEWS from
Gummer's How (1054 feet), and Finsthwaite Tower (605 feet).

ONE of the oldest Hostelries in the English Lake District, and patronised for over a century past by Royalty, Nobility, and Celebrities of the day, the good old fashioned style being studiously retained by the present Proprietor.   Boarding and week-end terms on application.

This favourite old Coaching House is one of the most charming Retreats in the Lake District, and the Tariff is so economically arranged as to offer facilities for families and parties desiring rest, recreation and pleasure, such as are offered by no other First-class Hotel in the English Lake District.   Every attention is paid to the Culinary department, being supplied by home farm produce. The Hotel is in the midst of a lovely country, well wooded, surrounded by hills, and within a few yards of the Lake.   For boating, free fishing, lovely walks and drives, and for retirement, this Hotel is unsurpassed in the district.

EDWIN WAUGH says—" Home-like and well furnished."   NATHANIEL HAWTHORNE says—" The gem of the Lakes."
GUIDES GENERALLY say—" One of the loveliest beauty spots."

THE LAKE SIDE HOTEL,
LAKE SIDE via ULVERSTON.

**South End of Windermere Lake, one minute's walk from Lake Side Railway Station and Steamboat Pier.
Robinson's Coaches in connection with the Furness Railway Company's Circular Tours.
Telegrams: "LAKE SIDE HOTEL, ULVERSTON."**

THE handsome and attractive looking Lake Side Hotel has recently passed into the
possession of Mr. and Mrs. Robinson, of whom the gentleman named is familiar already to the
majority of visitors to the district as the owner of the well-organised service of coaches and
char-a-bancs which traverse the most delightful regions of the picturesque and romantic English

Lakeland.   The hotel, situated at the south end of Windermere, is a commodious modern
building, designed throughout on the most up-to-date lines, comprising spacious and well-
appointed public and private rooms, with a number of airy and comfortably furnished bed-rooms
commanding charming views of the surrounding lake and mountain scenery.   Adjoining the
hotel are large premises used as temperance refreshment rooms, which provide excellent
accommodation for pic-nic and excursion parties whose catering will be a great feature of the
new management.   The hotel is undergoing a thorough renovation previous to Mr. and Mrs.
Robinson taking possession, and numerous improvements are in progress which will add
considerably to the comfort and enjoyment of visitors and tourists staying at the Lakeside
establishment.   A capital fleet of rowing and sailing boats is available at the pier attached to the
hotel, and as previously intimated this will be the starting place of Robinson's coaches and
char-a-bancs in connection with the two tours, the first to Esthwaite water and the Ferry circular
tour, and the other to Cartmel Priory and Newby Bridge.   Both Mr. and Mrs. Robinson enjoy
a wide measure of popularity with all classes of visitors, and in their new enterprise as proprietors
of one of the best and most comfortable hotels in the Lake district, carry with them the heartiest
good wishes of a wide circle of well wishers among those who have had past experience of their
abilities in catering for the enjoyment of the public.

BOWNESS.

PERHAPS the most popular Lake resort in the tourist and holiday season is the quaint and curiously constructed town of Bowness, which has been aptly described as a "labyrinth of small streets" of maze-like formation, containing however numerous excellent business establishments and pretty attractive villas and cottage residences, mostly available for the accommodation of the throngs of visitors and excursionists who make this their head-quarters in the summer and autumn months.

Bowness-on-Windermere, to give the full title necessary to distinguish it from another town of the same name in Cumberland, is recognised as the centre of the principal yachting and boating

BOWNESS PARISH CHURCH.

stations on the Lake, and is also the chief starting point of the delightful steam-boat trips by which the manifold and picturesque views of lake and mountain are unfolded to the visitor in all their varied beauty. During the season too, most of the principal yacht and boating regattas are decided off Bowness, and it is also the venue of many exciting swimming competitions, a favourite test of prowess of the contestants being their ability to make the circuit of Belle Isle, or cross the Lake at its widest part, a feat frequently accomplished by emulators of Leander's historic performance on the Hellespont.

An excellent service of omnibuses runs between Windermere and Bowness, and in the village is a capital institute, and a pretty church (St. Mary's), with tower, containing a sweet-toned peal of eight bells.

The church is worthy of more than a passing notice. It possesses topping its tower, one of those curious "Saddle-back" roofs so seldom seen in this particular neighbourhood. Architects are now making use of this particular form of tower termination. The new church at Flookburgh being one example; and the tower of Broughton-in-Furness church, now being erected at the cost of

THE FERRY, WINDERMERE.

HEAD OF WINDERMERE.

the Rt. Hon. Viscount Cross G.C.B., will have a like topping. In some parts of Wales this particular form of architecture is common.

The east window of the church, popularly, but wrongly, called the "Furness Abbey Window," is worth a close inspection. Tradition says that it once adorned the Abbey at Furness. This it certainly did not, but it is quite possible that it may once have done duty at Cartmel Priory. There is in the church a curious old bible and other books chained to a pillar.

We know no place more fitted for a busy man who can steal a few days at Easter or Whitsuntide, to seek enjoyment at, than Bowness. He can do just as much or as little as he likes, yet in either case can get amusement. It is one of the places of call of the steam-boats that ply up and down the lake so that a short sail will land him either at Ambleside or at Lakeside, or across the lake at the Ferry. There are many coaches prepared to take him to all points of interest in the Lake District, or, if he will, and if his legs are in good "fettle" as the country folk style it, he can make many pedestrian excursions varying his distance according to his inclination

BELLE ISLE, WINDERMERE.

yet always arriving at some point of interest. A sail to Ambleside and a long walk on, will land him over Kirkstone Pass into Patterdale and so on to Ullswater. It is a most delightful excursion, and the exhaustion caused by the steep climb up the Pass may be allayed by humble refreshment at the quaint little Inn that crowns the summit of the Pass, and claims, amongst many others, to be the highest inhabited house in the United Kingdom. A shorter walk, again from Ambleside takes him to Thirlmere, a lake in our estimation spoilt by the water-loving propensities of the Manchester Corporation. Some however profess to think that man's handi-work has improved Nature. Near the end of Thirlmere at a hamlet called Wythburn is a comfortable but small Inn, The Nag's Head. It is one of the best starting points for those who design to climb the "dark brow of the mighty Helvellyn." Across the lake is the tiny group of houses, ambitiously entitled "The City"—a name familiar to those who have studied Hall Caine's inimitable novel, "The Shadow of a Crime."

Crossing the lake from Bowness a long pull brings the wayfarer to the quaint old town of Hawkshead, whence the walk may be prolonged to Coniston.

WRAY CASTLE, WINDERMERE.

BOWNESS BAY AND OLD ENGLAND HOTEL.

THE "OLD ENGLAND" AND "ROYAL" HOTELS,

❧ WINDERMERE. ❧

Mr. ROGER BOWNASS, Proprietor.

Telegraphic Address—
"OLD ENGLAND, WINDERMERE."

Telephone Nos. 12 & 45.

THE proprietor of these establishments is one of the few private individuals in the kingdom who can claim the direct patronage of His Imperial Majesty, the Emperor of Germany, whose hereditary patriotism to the land of his royal grandparent, it may be naturally assumed, would attract his attention to a house bearing so national a title.

THE OLD ENGLAND HOTEL occupies a unique position, standing in its own charming grounds, extending to the private boat landings on the Lake side, and in the midst of the most beautiful and picturesque scenery in the world-famous lake district, within easy distance of the principal mountains, lakes and waterfalls. The hotel is a handsome and commodious structure of lofty elevation, the windows commanding varied and extensive views on all sides, and is furnished and decorated throughout in *recherché* modern style. The public apartments comprise elegantly appointed drawing room, large and lofty coffee room, well-equipped billiard room, sitting rooms, and a finely proportioned ball room, in which dances are frequently given in the season. There are also private apartments *en suite* and a number of single and double bed rooms, replete with all modern aids to convenience and comfort, in the form of bath rooms, lavatories, etc. Four-in-hand Coaches leave the Hotels daily for all parts of the district.

THE ROYAL HOTEL—which by the way, is the oldest in the neighbourhood, and, as its title suggests, has entertained celebrities of the highest distinction during its existence—is centrally situated, in close proximity to the Old England Hotel and Lake Windermere. The internal arrangements have been brought up to date during the recent work of improvement, among the new features being the addition of a spacious and lofty coffee room. The hotel has been re-furnished and re-decorated throughout, an electric light installation has been fitted, and the sanitary arrangements are completely in accordance with the most improved modern methods.

Mr. T. M. HOLMES,
DISPENSING AND PHOTOGRAPHIC CHEMIST,
Royal Square, BOWNESS=ON=WINDERMERE.

The present year, 1900, will celebrate the centenary of the above-named establishment, which may justly claim a record in the lengthened period the practice, now in the possesion of Mr. T. M. Holmes, has been in existence. Situated opposite the Royal Hotel, the premises have a handsome and attractive window frontage of plate glass, and are appointed throughout in modern style in harmony with the requirements of a high-class business of this character. The stock is of the most comprehensive and diversified nature, and comprises all the usual items in the form of drugs and chemicals for dispensing purposes, patent and pro-

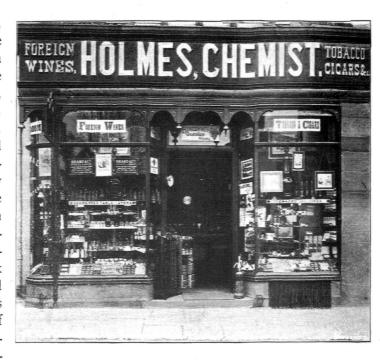

prietary medicines, pefumery, and requisites for the toilet, the nursery and surgical and medical practice. An important prominence is given to photographic supplies in the most approved appliances and accessories, and for the convenience of amateurs and the now universal Kodak operators, a specially fitted dark room is provided for developing negatives, Mr. Holmes is also a wine merchant and dealer in mineral waters, and a portion of the establishment is set apart for the sale of British and Foreign cigars, fancy packet tobaccos, pipes, and smoker's requisites of first-class quality supplied at popular prices. A branch shop has been more recently opened higher up the street, and this is similarly well stocked with a large assortment of goods in this line.

OLD ENGLISH LAVENDER WATER, bottles 1/-, 2/- & 4/6.

Windermere Bouquet, in bottles, 1/-, 2/6 & 4/6.

HOLMES' DIGESTIVE. A never-failing remedy for Indigestion, Dyspepsia, Heartburn, etc., in bottles 1/1½, large size 2/3.

ATKINSON'S

GROCERY STORES, ITALIAN WAREHOUSE, ✤ ✤ ✤
✤ ✤ ✤ AND LAKE DISTRICT BAKERY,

Royal Square and Lake Road, BOWNESS=ON=WINDERMERE.

ESTABLISHED in 1800, the business to which our notice refers, completes in the coming year the centenary of its establishment, and in the hands of its enterprising owner, Mr. Atkinson, enters upon a renewed lease of a successful career with the opening of the new era about to be inaugurated. Known as the Lake District Bakery, the establishment occupies a prominent site, and is arranged throughout on up-to-date lines, the electric light and all modern appointments being installed as aids to the efficient conduct of a large grocery and general purveying business. A noteworthy innovation has been introduced in the upper part of the premises, which has been converted into a tastefully and artistically decorated refreshment room, popularly known as the "Mikado Café," designed in Japanese style. This pretty

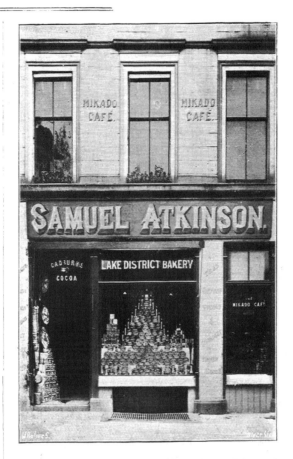

apartment is furnished with small tables and chairs, and here visitors are served with delicious coffee prepared from the fresh roasted berries, which are ground as often as required for each infusion. Accompanying this beverage is supplied a dainty delicacy in the form of Windermere "Ice" Cake, an ideal cake for afternoon tea. This is the local depôt for all the noted productions of Atkinsons of Windermere, the chief speciality of which is the **Windermere "Ice" Cake.**

The other specialities are:—

The Windermere Gingerbread,
Picaroon Cakes . . . .
Atkinson's Shortbread . .
Atkinson's Peppermint Creams,

all of which are in great demand in all parts of the country.

METCALFE'S LICENSED CRITERION CAFÉ,
Confectioner and Wine Merchant,
BOWNESS-ON-WINDERMERE.

SKILFUL and tasteful catering, combined with very moderate charges, is evidently appreciated by a large section of the holiday makers who resort to Windermere in the season, and whose increasing patronage of the Criterion Café is sufficient testimony to the proprietor's abilities in providing for the requirements of visitors. Centrally situated near the Royal Hotel and the quaint old Parish Church, Mrs. Metcalfe's establishment is exceedingly convenient, being only a minute's walk from the boat landings, and with its attractive double window frontage, offers hospitable invitation to the tourist on arrival. Here are served daintily prepared breakfasts, dinners, and teas, at popular prices. The Criterion Café is furnished in up-to-date style and is noted for the excellence of the teas, coffees, chocolate, etc. The establishment is licensed for the sale of wines, champagnes, ales, and stouts, the proprietress being agent for Messrs. W. & A. Gilbey, and the best brewers of malt liquors. Special arrangements are made for the entertainment of choir, school and picnic parties, who are catered for at moderate contract charges.

Mr. HORACE DAWES,
DEALER IN HIGH-CLASS WORKS OF ART,
Lonsdale Gallery,
BOWNESS-ON-WINDERMERE.

VISITORS to Bowness interested in art matters will find ample scope for enjoyment in an inspection of the well-known Lonsdale Gallery, where the spirited proprietor, Mr. Horace Dawes, has always on view a choice collection of examples of oil paintings, water colours and prints by eminent representatives of the ancient and modern schools, especially of those who selected the lovely Lake country as the scene of their labours. Mr. Dawes has been in the district as a dealer in high-class works of art, for the past quarter of a century, and about five years ago built his present gallery, named, by special permission, after the distinguished nobleman whose patronage has been so liberally extended to the Fine Arts, and whose princely seat is one of the show places of the locality. The establishment is of handsome appearance, is lighted by electricity, and affords admirable facilities for the display of the large and costly stock of pictures, antique china, silver, and old plate, miniatures, bric-a-brac, antique jewellery, and curios, with which the show-rooms are crowded. There is also a special room set apart for views

and photographs of the district, of which an extensive assortment is on view.

Established 1874.   Telegrams:—"NICHOLSON, BOWNESS, WINDERMERE."   Telephone No. 17.

Mr. JOHN NICHOLSON,

Auctioneer, Valuer, House and Estate Agent,
Lake Road, BOWNESS, Windermere.

VISITORS to the charming and picturesque districts of the Lake country, whether requiring temporary accommodation only or taking up a permanent residence, will find their convenience

studied by placing themselves in communication with Mr. John Nicholson, who has an extensive practice as house and estate agent, in addition to undertaking sales by auction and valuation of property of every description. This gentlemen has always on his books some hundreds of residences—furnished and unfurnished—in the most delightful sites in the district, a list of which is issued monthly, accompanied by a complete map of the Lakes of Cumberland, Westmorland, and Lancashire, and is forwarded free on application, with all requisite information as to rents, etc. Building land in various parts of the district may also be purchased through Mr. Nicholson's agency, plans and particulars of the Storrs Hall, Heathwaite, Holme Well, Gilpin Park, Tower Wood, and other estates being furnished on application. The offices are situate within five minutes' walk from the landing stage, and one mile from Windermere railway station, where Mr. Nicholson or his representatives may be consulted daily.

ATKINSON'S

General Drapery, Dressmaking, Millinery, Hosiery, Glove and Gent's Mercery Establishment.

West End House, BOWNESS=ON=WINDMERERE.

No better or more convincing evidence of the popularity of the Lake district as a holiday resort can be furnished than in the increasing prosperity of the trade of Bowness, of which an apt illustration is to hand in the case of West End House, where Mrs. Atkinson, the

proprietress, is now carrying out extensive enlargement of the premises in order to cope with the rapid expansion of her business. The establishment is of many years standing, and has always been noted for the freshness and variety of the goods supplied, the leading lines being

LATEST NOVELTIES IN MILLINERY,

Reproduced from the Season's New Models from London and Paris Designs.

Speciality : LADIES' SHIRTS, IN SILK, MUSLIN, AND COTTON.

Smart Tailor-made Costumes.   Waterproof Coats and Capes.

DRESSMAKING UNDER EXPERIENCED MANAGEMENT.

Complete Stock of Household Linen.   Furnishing Drapery.

Mr. GRAHAM J. ROBINSON,

General and Fancy Draper,

Royal Square, BOWNESS=ON=WINDERMERE.

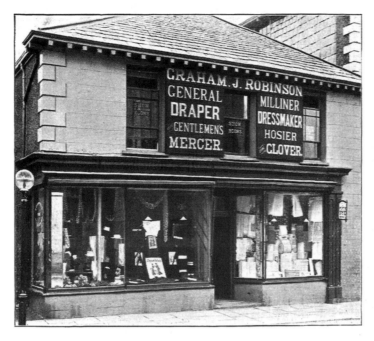

To the numerous visitors who throng the Lake country during the season, we can hardly suggest an establishment of greater convenience than that so ably and successfully conducted by Mr. Graham J. Robinson, whose business founded half a century ago is one of the oldest in this particular line in the district. The handsome shop, centrally situated in Royal Square, near the leading hotel, has an attractive double window frontage, in which is displayed with tasteful effect a large and varied assortment of the latest novelties and styles in dress fabrics, mantles, jackets, capes, fashionable millinery, flowers, feathers, gloves, ladies' underclothing, corsets, hosiery and general and fancy drapery of every description. The spacious interior, lighted throughout by an electric installation is conveniently arranged for the sale departments, and upstairs are show rooms for millinery, ladies' complete outfittings and a large stock of waterproof garments suitable for wear in the district. There are also work rooms in which several experienced hands are engaged in making up orders for ladies' costumes, millinery and family mourning, the latter being a leading speciality of the house.

Mr. F. W. TYSON,

PRACTICAL BOOT MAKER,

Lake Road, Bowness=on=Windermere.

THE perfection of easy-fitting and comfortable footgear may be implicitly relied upon when purchasing or ordering from Mr. Tyson's establishment, one of the most attractive and well-stocked boot and shoe warehouses in Bowness. Situated in the main thoroughfare, the premises have a neat modern window frontage, in which is displayed a tasteful assortment of novelties in ladies' boots and shoes in fashionable styles for the season's wear, and behind this is the well-appointed shop, fully stocked with a general selection of all kinds of gentlemen's and juveniles' goods in all sizes. A leading speciality, for which Mr. Tyson is sole agent, is the celebrated "K" make of pliant boots and shoes for light and easy wear, the "City," with anhydrous waterproof soles, and other types of this manufacture in a variety of patterns for

all seasons. Special attention is also given to the execution of bespoke orders for riding, hunting, fishing, and walking boots and shoes, in which the sound and reliable quality of the materials, and excellence of the workmanship and finish are a sufficient recommendation.

MR. H. NICHOLLS,

JEWELLER & SILVERSMITH,

BOWNESS, WINDERMERE.

PATRONISED by Royalty itself in the popular personality of H.R.H. the Prince of Wales, Mr. Nicholls' establishment may justly claim to rank with the most influential business houses in Bowness, where it was originally founded as far back as 1830. The windows, facing the main thoroughfare of the town, have a most attractive appearance, presenting to view a diversified display of elegant novelties in gold and gem jewellery, watches, clocks, antique silver plate, and other goods of a useful and ornamental character, suitably adapted for wedding and birthday gifts and souvenirs for all occasions. The interior of the establishment is handsomely appointed in modern style, lighted throughout by an electric installation, and replete with a splendid stock of valuable goods indicated in the preceding summary. Mr. Nicholls is also vendor of a very popular speciality of local significance in the "Ambleside" silver kettle, an article of original and unique design, exactly the thing for a reminder of a pleasant visit to the beautiful lake district, which gives it its title. Special attention is also bestowed on all kinds of watch, clock, and jewellery repairs, which are executed by practical workmen on the premises, and it should also be noted that Mr. Nicholls undertakes the winding of public or private clocks by contract.

Mr. WATERS,

General and Furnishing Ironmonger, Fishing Tackle Dealer,

Lake Road, BOWNESS-ON-WINDERMERE.

ALL the usual requisites supplied by such establishments are obtainable in the comprehensive and varied stock held by Mr. G. H. Waters, who combines with the business of a general and furnishing ironmonger, that of a glass and china and fancy goods dealer. The premises occupy a corner position in the main thoroughfare with a frontage of four plate glass windows in which is presented an attractive display of high-class goods, indicating the leading departments. The establishment is divided into two positions, of which the first is devoted to a large assortment of art metal goods in bronze, copper and brass, new designs in lamps, coal vases, and electro plate ware, table and pocket cutlery and every article and utensil required for culinary and domestic use, brushes, oils, paints, etc. On the other side are offered goods of a more decorative character, in glass, china, fancy ornaments, and a wide range of articles suited for the purpose of birthday and other gifts and souvenirs of a visit to the Lake district. There is an exceptionally choice assortment of photographic views which will well-repay inspecton.

MR. T. RUSSELL,

General Furnishing Ironmonger, Plumber, Heating and Hot Water Apparatus Engineer, Pneumatic and Electric Bell Fitter, Etc.,

Merton House, Lake Road, BOWNESS=ON=WINDERMERE.

Extending back nearly half-a-century since it was originally founded, Mr. T. Russell's business ranks as the oldest in the plumbing and kindred industries in the Windermere district, where he has established a wide-spread connection as a sanitary expert and a thoroughly practical all-round representative of the trade. As indicating the substantial nature of the

business, it may be mentioned that Mr. Russell has carried out the entire sanitary and plumbing work in connection with the Belsfield and Old England hotels, and within the last 30 years, has at various times entirely re-covered with lead the ancient parish church of Windermere. As a registered member of the Worshipful Company of Plumbers (London), he is qualified by examination to undertake all branches of sanitary work on the most improved scientific principles and is also largely engaged in contracts for heating public and private buildings, fixing hot water apparatus, electric bells, &c. Merton House is situated in Lake Road, Bowness, having a handsome double-window frontage in which is presented an attractive display of high-class art metal work, brass and copper goods, fireside suites, cutlery and electro-plate, gas and electric light globes and fittings, &c.; while inside the shop and store-rooms are to be found all the usual items that form the stock of an up-to-date ironmongery establishment.

Mr. Russell has for the past ten years been closely identified with the public life of the locality, and as a member of the Urban District Council has rendered invaluable service to his fellow ratepayers by his share in the administration of the affairs of the town.

MISS AINSWORTH,
Confectioner,
Kendal Road, BOWNESS-ON-WINDERMERE.

ALWAYS tastefully arranged, the window display at Miss Ainsworth's establishment, offers a tempting choice of high-class confectionery of the best English, Continental and American manufacture, with the accompaniment of light pastry and other comestibles and table dainties in great variety. The present premises, occupied by Miss Ainsworth for the past twelve months, are conveniently situated within three minutes walk of the Lake side, and comprise a compact and prettily appointed shop, with entrance adjoining to the private apartments, which are available for families and tourists visiting the district. The accommodation in this part of the establishment includes well furnished sitting and bed rooms, bath room and all modern conveniences, the entire arrangements being thoroughly home-like and comfortable, and the cooking and attendance everything that can be desired. The house is lighted throughout by electricity, and is scrupulously clean and well-ordered, Miss Ainsworth giving her close personal supervision to all matters of household management that can contribute to the convenience and enjoyment of her guests. Light refreshments may be obtained.

Mr. W. KELLETT,
VICTORIA FURNISHING STORES,
Lake Road, BOWNESS-ON-WINDERMERE.

EVERY article of household furnishing and requisites of all kinds for the equipment of a residence of any size may be obtained of first-class reliable quality and very reasonable prices at Mr. W. Kellett's well-stocked Stores, where he is showing one of the largest assortments of this class of goods in the Lake district. "The Victoria Furnishing Stores" are situated in Lake Road, and consist of a commodious shop and show-room with warehouse in the rear, lighted throughout by an electric installation, and affording much more space in the interior than the outward appearance would suggest. The display of goods is exceptionally varied, including some handsome new designs in drawing room suites, dining room and bed room appointments, brass and iron bedsteads, wire, hair, wool and straw mattresses and bedding, over-mantles, mirrors, carpets, rugs, oilcloths,

linoleums, glass and china, domestic and culinary utensils, wringing machines, mail carts, basinettes, and an extensive selection of art furnishings and decorative goods and paper

hangings at the lowest prices, Mr. Kellett is a thoroughly practical cabinet maker, upholsterer, paper-hanger, joiner and picture framer.

WINDERMERE.

ESSENTIALLY a development of the closing years of the century. The village, named after the most beautiful of English inland waters, is a creature of modern growth, and as a residential centre, either *en permanence* or for the holiday periods, has probably few contemporaries in popularity in the British Isles. Although bearing the name of the Lake, Windermere itself is situated a distance of a mile and three-quarters from the water side by road, but is more speedily accessible by several pretty by-paths shortening the journey by foot to a quarter of an hour, and affording many glimpses of the charming natural beauties of the Lake, and the surrounding picturesque mountain scenery.

AN ISLAND ON WINDERMERE.

The village occupies an elevated position some 500 feet above the level of the sea, and about 300 feet above the Lake, the site enjoying a reputation for salubrity unsurpassed by any locality in the district; and, thanks to the wisely discriminating judgment of the authorities, the sanitation is perfectly up-to-date, the water pure beyond reproach, and the lighting, provided by an electrical plant installation, completes a scheme of modern improvement which many more ambitious communities might envy.

From the historical point of view, Windermere is perhaps not strikingly remarkable, but in this respect it at all events possesses in Elleray and its woods a region of classic interest as the home of Christopher North, author of the *Noctes Ambrosianæ*, and witty contributor to " Maga " in the days when " Blackwood's " was enriched by the masterpieces of Professor Wilson and the contemporary *litterati* and poets of the period.

Windermere is the centre of many delightful walks and carriage drives, the latter well-served by the circular tour coaches daily available, while the pedestrian has a wide range of choice, including the ascent to the summit of Orrest Head, which attains an altitude of about 400 feet above the level of the village, reached by a winding pathway leading from a gateway on the side of the Windermere and Ambleside road, through Elleray woods. The toil of the ascent is well repaid by the magnificent view of lake, wood, and mountain, offering a superb panorama, which may readily be conceded as the finest in the kingdom.

A numerous fleet of handsome and well-formed sailing and rowing boats is provided for visitors and these are invariably manned by trustworthy and reliable hands experienced in Lake navigation.

Although Bowness does not boast of a plethora of historic or ancient objects of interest, visitors with a tendency to archæological research will find ample occupation in an inspection of the fine old Church dedicated to St. Martin, the patron saint of the weather, not by any

GENERAL VIEW OF WINDERMERE LAKE.

means an unimportant factor in the full enjoyment of a Lakeside trip. The edifice, of mixed architecture with a square tower stands in an ancient burying ground in which are some very fine old yew-trees, which tradition implies are of several centuries growth. The beautiful east window, originally placed in Furness Abbey, is one of the oldest in the country, and is designed with three lights in the centre representing the incidents of the crucifixion, said to be the finest of glass painting now extant its restoration in 1871 having been carried out under the superintendance of the Royal Society of Antiquaries. There are several mural monuments in the interior including one in memory of the learned Bishop Watson of Llandaff, whose remains are laid to rest in the churchyard. A new church (St. John's) has been erected in the Windermere Road, and there are also some handsome edifices occupied for worship by the Roman Catholic, Wesleyan, Congregational and other denominations. The town is lighted up by an electric installation, and other proofs of the public spirit of the local authorities are evidenced in the excellence of the water and sanitary systems, which are completely in accord with the most progressive ideas of the leading scientists on these questions.

WINDERMERE AND LANGDALE PIKES.

FERRY NAB, WINDERMERE.

Mr. GEO. H. BROCKBANK,

Photographic Artist,

The Windermere Studio, WINDERMERE.

THE handsome and well-equipped studio of Mr. Geo. H. Brockbank is one of the first objects to attract the visitor's attention when passing along the main road to the Lakes, a few minutes walk from the London and North Western station. This excellent corner site was selected by Mr. Brockbank for the erection of his establishment in 1899, and here he has built the handsome premises, specially designed for a modern high-class photographic studio. The ground floor is occupied as a shop with an attractive display of fancy goods, albums, plush and other frames, and a large assortment of photographic views of the beauties of "Lakeland." On the first floor is the spacious studio completely furnished, and elegantly appointed reception room. Mr. Brockbank has had a wide practical experience in the profession having been articled in one of the leading studios, and after an extended engagements in the North of Ireland and Manchester, commenced practice on his own account at Windermere, where he has found ample scope for his abilities in every branch of portrait and landscape photography. Special attention is given to groups and outdoor work, and also to repro-

ductions or enlargements from any photographs which are artistically finished in carbon, colours or black and white, and framed to order if required.

Mr. A. W. JOHNSON,

Printer, Publisher, Stationer, etc.

"Lakes Chronicle" Office, Caxton House, WINDERMERE.

Also at Caxton House, BOWNESS-ON-WINDERMERE.

THE only mid-week journal published in Westmorland is the "Lakes Chronicle," the best advertising medium and news organ published in the Lakes district. The "Lakes Chronicle," first published in 1875, has practically been in the hands of its present proprietor from 1877. At both the Bowness and Windermere shops the stock held is thoroughly representative, general and fancy stationery, and a great variety of useful articles suitable for gifts and souvenirs. There is also a large selection of local views, photographs, Guide Books and Maps of the district. The works are completely equipped with modern plant for the production of high-class printing, and experienced hands are employed. Bookbinding in all styles is undertaken. The shop in Windermere is situate near to Rigg's Windermere Hotel, the Post Office, and the Railway Station, and that at Bowness is near the old Parish Church, and the Old England and Royal Hotels, and not far from the Steamer Pier. Both establishments are fitted with electric light installations throughout.

THE WINDERMERE CAFE,

..... WINDERMERE.

Proprietor, M. BURRELL.

THE beauties of nature are doubtless very satisfying food for the mind, but the prudent tourist and sightseer makes sure of the more material sustenance of food and drink, without which the loveliest scenery is apt to pall. For this purpose, the Windermere Café is admirably equipped in all its arrangements, while its position, not five minutes from the railway station, and near the lake and all the principal objects of interest, makes it specially convenient for the visiting public. The building is new and well appointed, the furniture and fitments having been supplied by Mr. Arthur W. Simpson, of Kendal, and the building is effectively lighted by electricity. The greatest cleanliness prevails in all departments. All kinds of light refreshments are served at the shortest notice, including tea, coffee, and cocoa, bread and butter, buttered toast, toasted teacake, the famous Windermere "ice" cake in various flavours, sandwiches, meat pies, milk, aerated waters, bovril, lemon squash, and the like. Cold beef, boiled ham, chicken and ham, potted meat, eggs in different styles, stewed fruit, etc., are also provided at moderate charges. The special agency is held for the Windermere "ice" cakes just mentioned.

Mr. W. LEIGHTON,

Boot Maker,

43, Crescent Road, WINDERMERE.

ESTABLISHED nearly half a century ago, Mr. Leighton has successfully built up an extensive and substantial business connection among the local residents and the numerous season visitors to the Lake country, where his thorough mastering of his trade, and the invariable excellence of his goods have long been recognised by his customers. The handsome shop in Crescent Road is fitted in up-to-date style, lighted by electricity and well-appointed throughout presenting a very tasteful display of the latest styles in ladies' and gentlemen's boots and shoes for all wears and all seasons, and providing every convenience for fitting on in the utmost privacy. The business is both wholesale and retail, Mr. Leighton being district agent for the celebrated "K" make of boots including "Anhydrous Waterproofs," "Natural," and other brands of this easy-

fitting and durable foot gear. Special attention is devoted to the execution of orders for bespoke work in which the perfection of fit and easy wear is guaranteed, and equal care is given to repairs which are carried out on the premises by a staff of experienced and reliable hands employed solely in these departments,

Mr. H. B. DAWES,
Beef and Pork Butcher,
Wholesale and Retail Ham and Bacon Curer,
WINDERMERE.

PRACTICALLY a new department of this old-established business has been opened recently by Mr. H. B. Dawes, who at considerable cost has now added to his premises the necessary facilities for the production of smoked home-cured hams and bacon from the best Westmorland and Cumberland oatmeal-fed pigs. This branch of purveying is supplementary to an extensive trade as a wholesale beef and pork butcher, carried out for many years at the establishment, an up-to-date modern building with attractive frontage surmounted by a handsome coat of arms, and fitted throughout in high-class style with marble appointments, ice-chest cold rooms and an electric light installation. In the rear are the premises used as slaughter house, stores, and well-equipped smoking house, wherein the

hams and bacon are prepared on the most efficient methods. Besides these popular specialities Mr. Dawes is also noted for his "Windermere sausage," polonies, pure home-rendered lard, potted beef, brawn, corned beef, and such delicacies as Herdwick mutton, Isle of Wight lamb, and French calf sweetbreads.

Mr. R. H. BARKER,
Chemist and Druggist,
ACME HOUSE, WINDERMERE.

AFTER passing his examination as a member of the Pharmaceutical Society and fulfilling an appointment for some years as senior assistant with the well known Chemists, Messrs. Corbyn and Stacey, of London, Mr. Barker commenced practice on his own account at Windermere, where he has since established a large and successful business in ministering to the requirements of the local residents and visitors. In addition to the usual dispensing, which is very carefully and accurately carried out under his personal supervision, Mr. Barker has also on hand a large and comprehensive general stock of drugs and chemicals, surgical appliances, perfumery, mineral waters, toilet requisites, patent and proprietary articles, and complete outfits of apparatus and accessories for amateur and professional photography, for which a well-equipped dark room is provided. He has some favourite specialities of his own preparation in the "Lakeland Violet," and "Lake Lily" perfumes, whose delicious fragrance commends them to the popular appreciation of lady visitors. The establishment, occupying a commanding corner position in the main thoroughfare, is justly regarded as one of the show business places in the town,

AMBLESIDE, RYDAL & GRASMERE.

THROUGHOUT the Lake district there is no more charming or diversified scenery than that of Ambleside, one of the most popular holiday centres inland in the country. Reached from Windermere by a perfect road, level all the way, except for a short distance, a favourite route it need scarcely be said for the now ubiquitous cyclist. Ambleside is located on a lower ledge of Wansfell, on the border of a finely timbered valley, watered by a number of streams, of which the principal is the Rothay, which flows from Grasmere and Rydal Lakes and joins the Brathay from Langdale just before it enters Windermere.

Photo. by A. Pettitt.   GENERAL VIEW OF AMBLESIDE.

The main thoroughfare of the town, which now possesses nearly 3,000 inhabitants, contains some very attractive business places combining all the facilities for shopping in all departments of trade and purveying, and here also are situated the principal hotels and numerous high-class boarding houses providing excellent residential accommodation for families and tourists. The Salutation Hotel is the starting point also for Taylor's popular coaching trips, while the Old Bridge House is perhaps one of the most photographed objects in Lakeland.

There are two churches :—St. Mary's and St. Ann's and a Wesleyan chapel, and a short distance from the town is Holy Trinity Church at Brathay. St. Mary's was erected in 1854 on a site nearly in the centre of the valley, between the Knoll (the residence of the late Miss Harriet Martineau) and the lake, and contains a very fine group of stained glass windows, one having been presented by English and American admirers of Wordsworth as a tribute to the memory of the poet.   It is also remarkable as the scene of the rushbearing festival, which takes place annually in the church towards the end of June.   About three quarters of a mile distant is

Photo by Brunskill.   STOCK GHYLL FORCE.

Waterhead the boating head-quarters for the upper portion of the lake where every facility is provided for the safe enjoyment of this favourite form of amusement.   Apart from its numerous and varied waterside attractions Ambleside claims in the famous Stock Ghyll Force, one of the most beautiful and romantic waterfalls in England.   This is reached by a short lane leading into the park which brings the visitor into full view of the mountain glen enriched by foliage and vegetation of ever-varying tints through which the water is precipitated over the face of the rocks dashing with impetuous force over three leaps divided by projecting rocks from a height of seventy feet and flowing into the river below.   A small charge is made to visitors for viewing Stock Ghyll, the sum thus obtained being applied to the expenses of maintaining its surroundings in good repair.   Another enjoyable excursion is a walk round Loughrigg Fell, a rocky and fern-clad hill, the summit commanding extensive views of the beautiful district; and there are numerous other walks well within the compass of the average pedestrian that will well repay the exertion.

From Ambleside, too, it is but a short mile walk to Rydal, so closely associated with the poet Wordsworth and his numerous circle of literary friends and celebrities. Rydal Mount, the poet's later residence, where he died on April 23, 1850, is situated a short distance from the church, and is now occupied by Mr. J. Fisher Wordsworth, whose wife is a great-granddaughter of the poet. The pretty cottage is embowered amidst sylvan surroundings of clustering roses, jessamine and flowering plants, well meriting the description given by Miss Martineau as "a true poet's

Photo by Brunskill. OLD MILL, AMBLESIDE.

garden." Other places of interest in the neighbourhood are the pretty cascades, the Rydal Waterfalls, and just beyond the village the road skirts the eastern side of Rydal Water, one of the smallest, but unquestionably one of the most picturesque of our English lakes. About two miles beyond Rydal is Grasmere Lake, a sheet of water about a mile in length by half-a-mile in width, but having the extreme depth of 180 feet. In the centre is a pretty islet, surmounted by a group of dark fir trees, and from here should be viewed the circular vale of Grasmere, one of the most impressive and romantic landscapes in the whole of the Lake District.

GRASMERE, FROM WISHING GATE.

Photo. by T. Redhead

DOVE COTTAGE, GRASMERE.

STEPPING STONES, AMBLESIDE.

At Grasmere, as each August comes round it brings with it a day of great merriment. Far and near the fame of Grasmere Sports have spread. Originally patronised by the villagers, the farmers, and the local gentry, the gala has grown into a day of holiday for many outside the immediate neighbourhood. We remember it when it was frequented only by those living around and by the gentry who possessed carriages which enabled them to make a somewhat lengthy journey. The next development of the popular element consisted in running hired waggonettes and char-a-bancs at a certain price per head. More recently the Railway Company have taken the matter in hand and by means of " specials " both by way of trains and steamboats have enabled many to reach the scene of festivity to whom it previously was only a name. Although the èlite still favour it, the field is now greatly in request amongst Barrovians and others who discuss in language not always quite technical the merits of the various competitors—chiefly the wrestlers. The wrestlers, yes it is for its wrestling—wrusselling the country folk have it—that Grasmere holds its glory. Steadman v Logan—what scenes those words conjure up to the initiated! Their day may perhaps be almost over, but their names will live for ever in the country hearts. And

GRASMERE AND LOUGHRIGG TERRACE.

what exploits in pole jumping has not Grasmere seen! Woodburn, and Ray and Stones. They were veritable heroes with the ashen pole! And then the Guides' Race, the long weary climb up Silver-how and the mad and reckless rush downwards! No wonder Grasmere Sports have been and are still a popular outing. Nor must we forget the hound-trail, not that we ever saw much of it, for Grasmere Sports day is notoriously a day of driving rain and sheeted showers that does not conduce to a clear view of the distant hills. It is a good day to spend at Grasmere, provided you have made sure of your bed some weeks before, and do not mind paying for your enjoyment. We have paid, and paid gladly 4d. for a penny bottle of ginger beer on such a day. But then Hotel keepers must live and there are long months when the visitor is unknown in Lakeland, and the only customer is a stray farmer. Why this should be the case we do not know, for even in the darkest months there is a beauty in the mountain homes that exists nowhere else. And there is an absence of the noise and clamour of the summer season that should appeal to those who seek for rest and refreshment. The moral of all this is:—if you have a few days to spare, visit lakeland in the winter, and you will be repaid for your experiment.

Telephone No. 14.

THE WHITE LION HOTEL,

AMBLESIDE.

FIRST=CLASS FAMILY, COMMERCIAL AND POSTING HOUSE.

Proprietor: Mr. WILSON HARTLEY.

The recent improvements effected at that well-known and popular establishment, the White Lion, which includes a new wing with a fine dining-hall seating fifty guests, have rendered this one of the most comfortable and commodious hotels in the Windermere district.   The house has also

been re-furnished throughout and the entire arrangement over-hauled with a view to bringing the accommodation up-to-date with every requirement of a first-class modern family and commercial hotel.   It is centrally situated, looking towards the Lake, and contains in addition to the public apartments, good private sitting rooms and a number of spacious and comfortable bed-rooms, replete with every convenience for visitors to the hotel.   The cooking and service are of undeniable excellence, as are also the wines, spirits, malt liquors and cigars, which are carefully selected by Mr. Wilson Hartley, the proprietor.   Good stabling attached to the house is available for hiring vehicles for drives in the neighbourhood, and conveyances are despatched to meet all steamers at Waterhead, while seats for the coaches leaving daily for Keswick, Coniston, Langdale and Ullswater, and Rigg's Royal Mail and other coaches for Windermere and Grasmere, may be booked at the Hotel.

The posting department is an invaluable feature of the house, horses and vehicles of all kinds being provided for drives and excursions in this charming district.   Special arrangements can be made for large parties, terms and full particulars being furnished on application.

"WANSFELL TOWER,"
PRIVATE HOTEL AND DINING ROOMS, AMBLESIDE.

CYCLISTS and tourists visiting the romantic and picturesque district of Ambleside may be commended to make their headquarters at "Wansfell Tower," which has recently been diverted from its original purpose as a Roman Catholic seminary, to that of an excellent and commodious private hotel. Situated only five minutes' walk from the pier, the house is favourably located at the entrance to Ambleside, and is within a short distance of the shores of the Lake. The accommodation comprises well-furnished dining and drawing rooms, coffee room, private sitting rooms, and a number of comfortable bedrooms replete with every convenience. There is also a large public dining room capable of seating seventy guests, available for parties, and attached to the house is good stabling and lock-up store rooms for cycles and motors. The hotel is under the management of Mrs. Whillans and Miss Waller, who have had considerable experience in the business, and who make a special study of catering for all classes of visitors on the most reasonable and satisfactory terms.

Messrs. NICHOLSON & WEARING,
The Ambleside and District House and Property Agency,
RYDAL ROAD, AMBLESIDE.

THE majority of the most eligible residences in this delightful part of the Lake country will be found on the register of Messrs. Nicholson and Wearing, whose Ambleside and District House and Property Agency, established about two years ago, offers exceptional facilities for negotiating between owners and prospective tenants desirous of settling in the neighbourhood. The Ambleside Agency is under the personal direction of Mr. Chas. H. Wearing and is situated near the Post Office on the main road to Grasmere and Rydal. The firm have an extensive practice as auctioneers and valuers, undertaking also sales by private treaty, inventories of furnished houses, insurance agency, and all business incidental to these branches, while full lists of unfurnished and completely appointed residences are supplied on application, no enquiry fees being charged to clients in this department. Mr. C. H. Wearing also practices in his own profession as an architect and surveyor, possessing the necessary qualifications in each branch. All enquiries receive prompt attention, and in case of telegrams may be addressed in abbreviated form to "Wearing, Ambleside."

MR. T. B. ATKINSON,

MILLINER, LADIES AND GENTS' OUTFITTER, GENERAL DRAPER, SILK MERCER,

LAKE ROAD, AMBLESIDE.

ALL the latest and smartest novelties of the season are promptly reproduced in the tasteful display of new goods for ladies' wear shown at Mr. Atkinson's well-known drapery and outfitting establishment, one of the most attractive shops in the main thoroughfare of Ambleside. The

premises occupy a prominent corner position and are fitted in up-to-date form, the five plate glass windows offering an exceptional advantage in exhibiting the goods as represented in the sale and show-rooms of the spacious interior. In addition to a large assortment of general drapery, the stock includes the most fashionable models in ladies costumes, tea and dinner gowns, mantles, jackets and the latest London and Paris styles in high-class millinery, ladies' underwear and outfittings. An extensive connection is supplied among the resident gentry in the neighbourhood, and the establishment also, needless to add, largely participates in the custom of the numerous visitors to the Lake district during the season, Mr. Atkinson sparing no effort in catering for the requirements of his *clientele* in each department of his well-managed business.

In gents' hosiery and underwear is offered an excellent assortment of goods of the best makers, and attention may also be directed to a remarkably cheap line in business shirts of faultless cut and style. Knickerbocker and cycling hose, flannel shirts, sweaters, Cardigan jackets, under-vests and pants and sanitary underclothing, umbrellas and a great variety of travelling requisites for journeys by land and sea.

Mr. HERBERT BELL,

PHOTOGRAPHER,

AMBLESIDE.

RYDAL WATER.   GRASMERE.

BLEA TARN.   ULLSWATER.

OCCUPYING a central position, the studio of Mr. Bell is one of the best equipped and appointed in the district, wherein he has established a wide-spread and steadily growing practice as a skilful and accomplished representative of the photographic art. The establishment has an attractive double window frontage, in which is displayed a varied selection of exquisitely finished specimens in every style of portraiture, from the smallest vignette to the life-like enlargement, the latter being a speciality in carbon and platinotype, together with landscapes and local views of the lovely scenery and objects of interest for which the neighbourhood is famous. The studio itself is replete with all the most modern apparatus and accessories, and is personally attended to by Mr. Bell, who is an adept in the difficult art of posing, and every detail of the art that ensures the perfection of finish in either individual portraits or wedding, family or club groups, Mr. Bell has also a good show of prints, photographs of celebrities, etc., and supplies picture frames.

Mr. W. J. HIRD,

Watchmaker, Jeweller, Silversmith, and Optician,

MARKET PLACE, AMBLESIDE.

OF old-established and substantial standing, the business now conducted by Mr. W. J. Hird has for half-a-century maintained a leading position in the trade of the lake district, and is now recognised as the principal house of the kind in this locality. Centrally situated in the Market Place, near the Market Hall, the establishment has a handsome window frontage presenting an attractively displayed assortment of high-class goods in gold and silver watches, gem and gold jewellery, electro-plate and sterling silver ware, and a great variety of elegant and useful articles and novelties suitable for gifts and local souvenirs. A large stock is also held of optical goods, including spectacles and folders, field and opera glasses, for which the sight is accurately tested to suit the exact defect of the customer. An important and very successful department has also been established by Mr. Hird for re-plating or repairing of table plate, and the loan of plate and cutlery on hire, which is replete with an immense variety of goods specially adapted for use and display either at large banquets or private dinner parties. This system will be found of exceptional advantage to entertainers on any scale, who at almost nominal charges can supplement their table resources with requisites in the form of high-class furnishings of artistic design, from the smallest article in use to the most elaborate pieces for side-board decoration.

Messrs. W. & J. ASPLIN,

BUTCHERS, POULTERERS AND BACON CURERS,

CHURCH STREET, AMBLESIDE.

TELEPHONE: No. 9.

ESTABLISHED exactly a century ago, the business of Messrs. W. & J. Asplin can undoubtedly claim to rank as one of the oldest purveying concerns in Westmorland, and under the direction

of its present proprietors, has, during the past twenty years, largely extended a high-class influential family trade having connections throughout the district. The premises in Church Street are quite modern in appearance, and are fitted throughout in first-class style with white tile decorations and handsome appointment in marble slabs, etc., the whole presenting a perfectly cleanly and well-ordered neatness of arrangement indicating the care and attention devoted to these details. The quality of the purveying is of the highest, the firm buying invariably in the best markets, and as all meat is slaughtered in the premises, and kept in a well-equipped refrigerator, the primest condition is ensured in every joint or article of poultry sent out, Messrs. Asplin are noted for a speciality in their delicious mountain mutton which is supplied to customers in all parts of the country, as are also their choice home-cured hams and bacon, and spiced beef and pickled tongues of unrivalled quality as table delicacies. They are also breeders of hackneys, in which they have secured several prizes at the leading horse shows in the county.

Mr. JAMES ELLIOTT,
Bespoke Boot Maker and Repairer,
Market Place, AMBLESIDE.

As the recognised depôt for the widely celebrated "K" boots for all seasons and all wearers, Mr. Elliott's establishment is noted for the excellent quality of the goods supplied, not only in the speciality thus referred to, but alike in the reliable articles of his own make which he keeps in stock. The shop is centrally situated in the Market Place, a capital position for the business, and has a neat window frontage in which a varied assortment of novelties is displayed in the form of fashionable footgear for ladies', gentlemen's and children's wear. The stock also includes boots and shoes especially suitable for mountain climbing and tourists, in which an easy and comfortable fit is a *sine qua non* in actual wear. Special attention is bestowed upon orders for measured boots and shoes, for which lasts to fit each foot are made, and which in quality of material, workmanship and stylish finish are unsurpassed by any maker in the district. An extensive connection has been established by Mr. Elliott within the past few years, his customers including many of the resident gentry and influential visitors to this part of the Lake country.

Mr. HENRY HIRD,
Watchmaker, Goldsmith, Stationer, and Dealer in Fancy Goods,
KELSICK ROAD, AMBLESIDE.

PASSING by way of the main thoroughfare from the town to the Lake, it would be difficult to mention a more attractive feature than the handsome new premises opened by Mr. Henry Hird, Watchmaker, Goldsmith, etc., who has inaugurated for the first season of the century an entirely modern establishment, up-to-date in every detail of appointment and arrangement. The pretty window frontage is tastefully dressed with a choice selection of watches, clocks, diamond and gem jewellery, artistic engagement rings. Standard gold wedding rings and keepers, silver and electro plate ware, bronzes, optician's goods, and a great variety of articles of a useful and ornamental character, suitable for wedding and birthday gifts, presentation or prizes. There is also a complete stock of plain, fancy, and mercantile stationery, views of the district, and leather goods, purses, bags, and the nic-nacks which invite attention. As a thoroughly practical mechanical expert, Mr. Hird undertakes the repairing and adjustment of watches, chronometers and the most complicated movements, and has every facility for the execution of electro-plating and gilding, all these branches being carried out on the premises by experienced workmen under his close, careful supervision on very reasonable cash terms.

Mr. J. LONGMIRE,

𝔉amily 𝔊rocer and 𝔓rovision 𝔇ealer, 𝔅aker and Confectioner,

CENTRAL BUILDINGS, AMBLESIDE.

ONE of the best known establishments in the purveying trade in Ambleside. Mr. Longmire's well-stocked shop is widely noted for the high standard of quality of the goods supplied in each

department of a high-class grocery and provision business. This was started some ten years ago by the present proprietor, who by dint of energetic and judicious management has secured an extensive measure of substantial support in the locality. The stock is well-selected and comprises general groceries and Italian warehouse goods of all the leading brands, together with highly appreciated specialities in home cured hams, Wiltshire smoked bacon, Stilton and Wensleydale cheeses and other English and imported provisions of primest quality. Bread baking and confectionery form an important branch of the business, ovens built on the most approved principle having recently been added, thereby placing this branch well to the front. Family orders are collected and delivered to customer's own residences, and special and careful attention is given to their execution, the proprietor personally exercising the closest supervision over every detail of the business to ensure efficiency and promptitude in all transactions,

DALTON-IN-FURNESS.

IT is an ancient town, once regarded as the capital of Furness; but after the dissolution of Furness Abbey, the supremacy was acquired by Ulverston. Of late years, owing to the development of the mining industry, its population has largely increased. The main thoroughfare of Dalton rises by a gradual ascent to the market place, in which there stands a plain cross of limestone, placed upon an octagonal limestone pedestal. This was erected by the late Duke of Buccleuch, the lord of the manor. Just beyond it there stands an oblong tower called the Castle, being all that remains of a much more extensive structure. It is built of limestone and sandstone, and is surmounted by a parapet, at the angles of which are marble statues. The object of its erection was probably to afford defence against the predatory incursions of Scottish freebooters, to which for some centuries the northern counties were con-

Photo by Hargreaves.   DALTON CHURCH.

stantly subject. The present building probably dates from the reign of Edward III., but it is supposed to occupy the site of one much earlier. The Parish Church of Dalton, dedicated to St. Mary, is situated on the declivity of a hill in the immediate vicinity of the Castle. The ancient church is known to have existed in the year 1200. It was rebuilt in 1826, and it underwent further improvement in 1832. But in 1884-5 it was entirely removed, and a handsome edifice was built upon the site of the old church, Messrs. Paley & Austin being the architects. It consists of nave, chancel, and aisle, with a lofty tower, and is built of red sandstone, quarried in the district. It contains some handsome stained glass windows, and an ancient font, said to have been brought from Furness Abbey. The cost of the new church was upwards of £10,000. The tower is a conspicuous object as seen from the railway. In the church is a stone erected to the memory of George Romney, the celebrated painter, who was born in this parish.

Mr. ROBERT BLAKE,

Printer, General Stationer, Bookbinder, Emigration Agent, etc.,

Market Street, DALTON-IN-FURNESS.

ESTABLISHED 1868.

VERY comprehensive in the scope of its operations, Mr. Blakes' business includes in its leading departments the execution of letterpress, lithographic printing, bookbinding, etc. The establishment has for many years been the publishing office of the "Dalton Parish Magazine," "North Lonsdale Congregational Magazine," "Through Furness to the English Lakes," also Book of Views, "Dalton and Furness Abbey." The premises, situated in Market Street, have an attractive window frontage, in which is displayed for inspection a varied assortment of goods of a useful and artistic character including a large selection of pretty views of local places of interest, and other articles suitable for gifts, souvenirs, etc. Mr. Blake is also a dealer in cycles, sewing machines, musical instruments and picture frame manufacturer. Orders in the various branches of trade carried out on the premises in a reliable and workmanlike manner at reasonable charges.

Mr. Blake is authorised government emigration agent for the district, tickets being issued for all Steamship Lines at this establishment for all parts of the world, and the fullest information is imparted on matters connected with passages to the Colonies or elsewhere. Mr. Blake enjoys about the largest connection in Shipping matters of any one in North Lancashire. It has often been said that passengers who have passed through his agency may be found in every part of the Globe. He stocks every requisite for use of the Emigrant and the Travelling Public.

For some years Mr. Blake owned the *Barrow Herald* but this he disposed of to advantage, in order to have more time at command for his Dalton duties.

He has held almost every position of honour in his native town, having had a seat on the School Board for 21 years. He is a member of the Board of Guardians, Secretary to the Sick Nursing Association, Secretary of the St. John Ambulance Classes, etc., and always found taking an active part in the various organizations of the town.

Mr. T. C. HOSKINS,

Artistic, General & Commercial Printer, Stationer, etc.,

Tudor Square, DALTON-IN-FURNESS.

EXCEPTIONAL facilities for the execution of printing in all its branches are provided at the well-equipped works of Mr. T. C. Hoskins, in Tudor Square, Dalton, where he has all the requisites in plant and up-to-date appliances for promptly getting out orders in every style of letterpress or lithographic work on the shortest notice. At the Tudor Square establishment is kept a large stock of general and commercial stationery, well-bound works by standard authors and popular writers on all subjects, an extensive assortment of fancy goods, views, photographs, etc., and other useful and decorative articles in great variety. A department is also established for supplying all the leading London and provincial journals, magazines, periodicals, etc., which are delivered at customers' residences as soon as received by the early morning trains. Orders for artistic, general and commercial printing, are undertaken at exceedingly reasonable charges, in any style of plain or displayed work, for which the services of experienced and reliable hands are employed in the works, and it should also be mentioned that bookbinding is another department of the business which claims the proprietor's attention.

Mr. H. B. ARMISTEAD,

FAMILY AND DISPENSING CHEMIST,

Market Street, DALTON-IN-FURNESS.

A VERY substantial old established pharmaceutical practice is conducted by the above named gentleman, who for twenty years has enjoyed a leading position both in his professional capacity as a dispensing and family chemist, and as a manufacturer of aerated waters of superior quality. Situated in the principal thoroughfare, Mr. Armistead's establishment has a plate glass window frontage in modern style and a well-furnished interior completely stocked with the best and freshest drugs and chemicals for compounding physicians prescriptions, etc., which are accurately prepared and registered, patent and proprietary articles by makers of repute, genuine horse and cattle medicines, perfumery, toilet and invalids requisites, and petroleum, colza, sperm and other oils and drysaltery of every description, Mr. Armistead is also agent for Messrs. W. and A. Gilbey's well-known brands of wines and spirits, and in connection with this department has a capital selection of choice British and foreign cigars, tobacco, snuff, etc. A first class plant is installed for the manufacture of aerated and mineral waters, for

which an extensive demand exists in all parts of the Furness district.

FURNESS ABBEY.

THE visitor, leaving Dalton, passes through a short tunnel, and cannot fail, as he proceeds along the line, to notice the park-like scenery of the vale through which he passes. On the left he will notice Abbots Wood, the mansion occupied for many years by the late Sir James Ramsden, and on an eminence to the left he will see Millwood, the residence of Edward Wadham, Esq., J.P. And soon he will notice on the right, in close proximity to the railway, the ruins of Furness Abbey, a house which once took rank among the grandest of English monastic buildings. Close by is the railway station and a hotel. This abbey was founded by a body of Lavignian monks who left Savignay in the year 1124, and made their temporary abode at Fulkett near Preston on the banks of the Ribble. Stephen count of

ABBOTS WOOD.

Boulogne and Mortain and afterwards King of England became their benefactor, and bestowed upon them by a charter dated in 1127 all his possessions in Furness, with the exception of the lands of Michael de Fleming, for the purpose of erecting and endowing an abbey for these monks who shortly afterwards forsook Fulkett and removed to this spot called the valley of Deadly Nightshade. The estates of the monks were increased from time to time by numerous gifts, and they acquired great power and wealth. In 1148 the Savignian Order became incorporated with the Cistercian Order, and in a few years, with some reluctance that rule was adopted by the monks of Furness. Little more is known of its history during its prosperous period than the record of the acquisition of lands and privileges, and of disputes with neighbouring landowners. At the dissolution of the Abbey in 1537, its yearly revenues amounted to about £900, being equal to about £9000 at the present day. It is now a most picturesque ruin. The conventual church is cruciform; the interior length is 280 feet, the width of the nave with aisles 65 feet and the width across the transepts from north to south 129 feet. From the centre of the

FURNESS ABBEY.

transept the great lantern tower arose, supported on four arches of which only one having an altitude of 52 feet now remains. The length of the chancel is 60 feet, and its breadth 30 feet.

FURNESS ABBEY, WEST TOWER.

The east window has been a magnificent specimen of perpendicular architecture, 47 feet high, but the arch is broken and there have been other windows. The walls are strengthed by large buttresses at the angles and between the windows. On the south side of the chancel are the sedelia, having four seats, with canopies beautifully executed in decorated style. On the floor of

CHAPTER HOUSE DOORWAY, FURNESS ABBEY.

the chancel are numerous ancient monuments. At the west end of the church is the belfry tower with walls eleven feet thick and supported by buttresses. It is of much later date than the rest

FURNESS ABBEY LOOKING WEST.

of the church. The south wall of the nave is standing but nearly the whole of the north wall has been destroyed. On the east of the north transept are three chapels, and two other chapels and

FURNESS ABBEY HOTEL.

only a few minutes by train, it adjoins the station, a covered way from the principal entrance leading directly to the down platform.

The Tariff is on a very reasonable basis, and the wines list comprises all the best brands from Messrs. Spiers and Pond's noted stock.

DRAWING ROOM, FURNESS ABBEY HOTEL.

the sacristy are attached to the south transept. In the cloister court the most noticeable feature is the three transitional arches, the heads of which form complete semicircles. The middle arch introduces us to a porch with a grained roof leading to the chapter house, a most beautiful specimen of early English architecture. Adjacent to the three great arches are two smaller ones, also round-headed, by which we enter the refectory. A range of lancet windows above it shows the remains of the dormitory. At the south end of the refectory are two roofed-in apartments, one of which is supposed to have been a chapel. At the opposite extremity of the Abbey grounds adjoining the railway station, there is another chapel called the gateway chapel. It is roofless. Close beside it stand two arches of modern construction. The ruins of the Abbey are now the property of the Duke of Devonshire. It is however but a very brief account that can here be given of the remains of Furness Abbey, and we can only state that the Abbey grounds comprised an area of 65 acres, and that in its prosperous days the abbots maintained a military force of 1200 men, and exercised supreme jurisdiction in Furness. The adjoining hotel affords ample accommodation for visitors; some interesting sculptures from the Abbey will be found inserted in the walls of different apartments. One of these is in the coffee-room. It represents in bas-relief the creation of Eve. Others are the woman with the issue of blood touching the hem of Christs' garment, Mary wiping His feet with her hair, St. John the Baptist, and St. John the Evangelist.

THE SEDELIA, FURNESS ABBEY.

Adjoining the ruins, in fact built upon a portion of them and surrounded by the grounds is the Furness Abbey Hotel, we have no hesitation in saying that visitors to the Lake District, cannot do better than arrange for a short stay in this beautiful and comfortable Hotel, to say that it is in the hands of Messrs. Spiers and Pond Ltd. is a guarantee not only for its good management, but that its cuisine is unexceptional; if a further proof were necessary it would be found in the fact that all the principal dinners in the district take place within its walls. The House itself is worthy of notice, it contains some noble rooms, more especially the coffee room and small dining rooms. The Hall too is a distinctive feature having lately been turned into a comfortable and graceful lounge, very comfortable Reading, Smoking and Billiard Rooms, and Ladies' Drawing Room. The bed-rooms are spacious and airy and overlook the grounds. The fire which unfortunately broke out some time ago and which gutted the larger portion of the house has now resulted in a beautiful and up-to-date decoration, and has also given the opportunity for a considerable re-arrangement, in fact the Hotel is now replete and up-to-date in every respect, and with its picturesque surroundings forms one of the most delightful provincial Hotels in the Country. It is within touch of Barrow by Tram Car and

Messrs. LOWDEN & POSTLETHWAITE,

AGRICULTURAL AND GENERAL AUCTIONEERS, ARBITRATORS, VALUERS, AND PROPERTY AGENTS,

The Barrow and County Estate and Auction Rooms,

CORNWALLIS STREET, BARROW-IN-FURNESS.

A VERY wide scope of operations characterises the above business, which, without question, is the largest of its class in the Furness district. Originally established in 1869, a prominent position has always been held in the community. At the present time very superior and admirable premises are

VIEW OF SALE ROOM.

occupied in Cornwallis Street, the building known as the Barrow and County Estate and Auction Rooms being three storeys in height and fitted with all the requisites of a first-class establishment of the kind, and the position (close to the Town Hall and facing the market) being central and accessible. The firm have had a particularly valuable experience in all branches of the profession, and are prepared to undertake everything coming under their range of activities. As set forth, they are agricultural and general auctioneers, arbitrators, hotel valuers, farm valuers, fire assessors, and house and estate agents. All business of the kind which may be placed in their hands is sure to receive the most scrupulous attention, and their long experience enables them to guarantee the most satisfactory results. They also go in largely for disposing of household and general furniture and effects, stocks in trade, machinery, farm stocks, implements, and the like. A number of important insurances agencies, etc., are held, among them that for the Hand in Hand Insurance Co., for the insurance of house property, stocks, furniture, and live and dead farming stock ; the Law Guarantee and Trust Society, for insuring hotels and beerhouse licences; and the Railway Passengers' Insurance Co., for insurance against accidents of all kinds. They are also agents for the Horse, Carriage, and General Insurance Co., for insurance against accidents and disease of cattle, sheep, pigs, farm and posting horses, entire horses, and also against drivers' accidents. The firm's connection is a large and widely extended one, among their clients being many of the landed proprietors of the district, as well as the principal farmers, business men, etc. All communications receive prompt attention.

CONISTON.

THE village of Coniston, or Church Coniston as it is more correctly termed, is situated at the head of the Lake that now bears that name. The village forms the termination of the branch of the Furness line that deviates from the road to Whitehaven at Foxfield, and after passing in turn through Broughton, Woodland and Torver, finally lands the wayfarer in the romantic valley of Coniston. The station bears a business-like appearance, as it is an emporium for the timber industry of the district, and also a depôt for the slates, that are quarried and fashioned in the immediate vicinity. The Copper Mines that date from the time of the Romans are now of small commercial value. Coniston is a convenient centre from which to visit Dungeon Ghyll, a waterfall of more than local

COTTAGE AT YEWDALE.

fame, and one that bears the impress of Wordsworth's appreciation. Brantwood the seat of the late Mr. Ruskin is just opposite to the station, on the further side of the lake, and the mortal remains of the loved Philosopher sleep in the peaceful churchyard of the village. Coniston Hall, on the margin of the lake is still an object of interest, with its beautiful old round chimneys and massive walls. It was for long the seat of the Flemings or Le Flemings, competing with Rydal Hall for their favours. It came into the family in the reign of Henry III. by the marriage of Sir Richard le Fleming with Elizabeth, daughter and heiress of Adam de Urswick. Since the time of the famous Sir Daniel le Fleming (1650-60), Coniston Hall has lapsed into the condition of a farm house.

Photo. by J. Redhead.   YEWDALE BECK, CONISTON.

TYSON'S WATERHEAD HOTEL,

CONISTON LAKE, LANCASHIRE.

Mr. J. TYSON, Proprietor.

THE holiday seeker desirous of exploring the manifold delights of the English Lake districts will find no more central nor convenient quarters than the Waterhead Hotel, a high-class establishment, occupying one of the most charming sites on the shores of Lake Coniston. The house is readily accessible by rail, an omnibus meeting all trains at the station, and contains

several large and handsomely furnished public apartments, including fine coffee room, ladies' drawing room, a well-appointed billiard room, private sitting rooms, and a number of airy and comfortable bed rooms, the windows of which command splendid views of the Lake and mountain scenery on all sides. The establishment stands in its own extensive and beautifully laid out pleasure grounds, several acres in extent containing well-sheltered walks, from which may be viewed Brantwood, the romantic home of the late John Ruskin, and Tent Lodge, for some time a favourite residence of the late Lord Tennyson. Stretching down to the water side, the visitors have every facility for boating and fishing, and a steam gondola runs daily on the Lake during the season. The stabling attached to the establishment is well provided with excellent vehicles, available for drives to all points of interest in the neighbourhood, and from here may also be obtained sure-footed mountain ponies for excursions up the hills. There are coaches daily to Ambleside and Windermere, and a coach leaves Coniston for Grasmere *via* Red Bank, at 10 a.m. every morning, returning by way of Ambleside, and embracing some of the finest scenery on this famous route. Among the excursions that may be made from the hotel are, round Coniston Lake, to Yewdale, Tilberthwaite Ghyll, Langdales, Blea Tarn, Dungeon Ghyll, round the Duddon Valley, Skelwith Force, Wray Castle, Furness Abbey, Tarn Hows, High Cross, Esthwaite, Lake Ferry, Grasmere, Ambleside, Hawkshead, and Belle Grange. The postal address is Coniston, R.S.O., Lancashire, and the telegraphic address, "Waterhead, Coniston," where all communications to Mr. J. Tyson, the proprietor, receive prompt attention.

The Ravenglass and Eskdale Railway.

A ROUTE scarcely so well known as its numerous attractions merit is that traversed by the Ravenglass and Eskdale Railway, a narrow gauge system which, between Ravenglass and Boot, opens up some of the most picturesque views of the mountain range dominated by Scafell and his gigantic neighbours. Commencing our journey at Ravenglass, we soon reach the little station at Eskdale Green, from whch a road runs south to Ulpha Bridge near Devoke Water. This is a tarn about half a mile long, celebrated for its red trout,

STANLEY GHYLL.

and containing a small island, the retreat of a colony of birds styled the Devoke Water mews, whose resentment at the presence of strangers is marked by their amusing cries and gyrations. Proceeding on our way we arrive at the pretty village of Boot, which may be strongly recommended as an ideal spot for a summer holiday, and which possesses all the advantages of pure air, good fishing in the rivers Esk and Mite, and is near to the grand scenery in and around Wasdale which includes Wastwater, the deepest lake in England. Among the objects of attraction to visitors are Birker Force and the famous Stanley Ghyll, or Dalegarth Force. The first named fall has its source in a small tarn on the western side of Birker Fell and has a cataract of sixty feet in height. This however cannot compare in rugged grandeur with Stanley Ghyll. It is about half an hour's easy distance from Boot and is situated in a deep and thickly wooded ravine, admission to which is obtained on application at a cottage near Dalegarth Hall. No more graphic pen picture of the beauties of Stanley Ghyll can be advanced than the description given by that gifted writer Miss Harriet Martineau, who pronounced it "the finest in the region." Entering the ravine at the bottom the stranger enjoys, for a short distance, a shaded walk by the brook side, thence gradually ascending by winding paths and rustic bridges, passing on his way numberless small falls, which add beauty to the scene, he reaches the principal fall. Here, amid a wilderness of ferns and wild flowers, he may sit in the cool, damp abyss, watching the fall of the waters into their clear rocky basin till his ear is satisfied with their dash and flow and his eye with the everlasting quiver of the ash sprays and the swaying of the young birches, which hang over from the ledges of the precipice. The height of the fall is about sixty feet, the stream issuing from a deep fissure in a perpendicular rock,

Photo. by A. Pettitt. BOOT, ESKDALE.

and leaping at one bound into the pool beneath.

There are many other places of interest in Boot and its vicinity, notably, the remains of

Photo. by A. Pettitt. GLEN ULPHA, ESKDALE.

Photo. by A. Pettitt.   HARD KNOTT PASS, UPPER ESKDALE.

the Roman Camp on Hard Knott, accessible by the Ravenglass and Eskdale Railway, which should certainly extend the growing popularity of this excellently organised system.

Photo. by A. Pettitt.   BRIDGE AT DALEGARTH, ESKDALE.

BRANTWOOD, RESIDENCE OF THE LATE PROFESSOR RUSKIN.

SEASCALE ^{AND}_{ITS} GOLF LINKS.

SEASCALE has, within the last few years, become a watering-place of some extent, and is rapidly growing in favour.   The air is magnificent and its bracing and invigorating qualities are

unequalled on the West Coast, also its close proximity to some of the best parts of the lake district adds to its popularity as visitors can enjoy both sea air and mountain scenery.

Photo. by J. Redhead.

WASTWATER WITH GREAT GABLE AND PART OF THE SCREES.

Wastwater is about 8 miles from Seascale.   The road passes through Gosforth, which is noted for the ancient cross in the churchyard.   This cross is 15 feet high, and is covered with carvings, which are thought to represent the triumph of Christianity, shown by means of the old Scandinavian legends.

There is one great objection to Seascale as a holiday resort. The mixture of sea and mountain air creates an appetite that taxes the resources of a man of moderate means to allay. Some people perhaps, would regard this as a recommendation, since it is a sign of vigorous health. There are people who tire of attempting to discover the secret of what the 'sad sea-waves are saying.' To such we recommend Seascale, for a walk or a drive inland speedily

Photo. by J. Redhead. STRANDS, NETHER WASDALE.

brings them into the wildest and most romantic scenery that England can boast. They can enjoy nature in her most fantastic mood, they can study primitive life and primitive customs to the full, and return with intellects refreshed to the unanswerable question. Not that the waves at Seascale reveal much of sadness. They are rather frisky or boisterous, and even at times passionate, they relinquish sleepy lapping and sullenness to their sisters in more southern seas.

. . THE GOLF LINKS. . .

Are the finest in the county, a splendid stretch of moor land upon the cliffs over-looking the sea, they are close to the town and are frequented by lovers of the game from all parts.

ST. BEES.

THE parish of St. Bees, including five chapelries and the important town of Whitehaven, is the most extensive in the County of Cumberland. St. Bees itself is a small town on the coast, and is of considerable antiquity. Its name is derived from St. Bega, an Irish princess, who founded a nunnery on the site of the present Church about the year 650. This was destroyed by the Danes; but about 500 years after the original foundation, in the reign of Henry I., it was replaced by a cell for a prior and six Benedictine monks under the Abbey of St. Mary, at York. This restoration was due to William des Meschines, brother of

Photo by A. Pettitt.   ST. BEES HEAD.

Ranulph des Meschines, first Earl of Cumberland. The conventual church, built of red sandstone, still stands, and retains some parts of the original edifice in connection with re-constructions. These original parts are of Norman architecture. The Church is cruciform in shape, and over the intersection is a low square tower. The ancient chancel had been unroofed for more than 200 years when it was renovated in 1810, and adapted as a college for theological students intending to enter the ministry of the Church of England. There is a Grammar School near the Church, founded by Archbishop Grindal in 1587. St. Bees Head is a bold promontory projecting about a mile into the sea, and rising from the water to a height of more than 300 feet.